The Violin

Keynote Books

By Bill Ballantine: THE VIOLIN
THE FLUTE
THE PIANO

Forthcoming Titles:

THE CLARINET

THE GUITAR

THE TRUMPET

DRUMS AND OTHER PERCUSSION INSTRUMENTS

THE CELLO

THE SAXOPHONE

THE TROMBONE

THE HORNS

THE OBOE

THE VIOLA

A KEYNOTE BOOK

The Violin

An Introduction to the Instrument

by Bill Ballantine

Franklin Watts, Inc.
845 Third Avenue
New York, N.Y. 10022

The author gratefully acknowledges kind assistance in the writing of this book given by Mary Canberg, violin teacher, Alexander Schneider, violinist and conductor, James Oliver Buswell IV, violinist, Jerry Juzek, violin maker, Ralph Gleason, jazz music authority, Harry A. Duffy, dealer in antique violins, with a special bow to Charlotte Russell, and Marion Wurlitzer of Rembert Wurlitzer, Inc.

*
787.1
B188
A-1

PHOTO CREDITS:

Rembert Wurlitzer, Inc. (Frontis., pp. 17, 46, 47, 54, 55, 56, 57, 67)
RCA Records (p. 21)
Christian Steiner (p. 29)
Hurok Concerts, Inc. (p. 26)
Metropolitan Museum of Art (p. 50)
Metropolitan Museum of Art, The Crosby Brown Collection of Musical Instruments, 1889 (pp. 37, 38, 40)
Bettmann Archive (pp. 62, 79)
Columbia Broadcasting System (p. 72)
Library of Congress (pp. 74, 75, 77, 81, 82, 88, 89, 90, 92)
Decca Records (p. 92)

SBN: 531-01845-8
Library of Congress Catalog Card Number: 75-115772

Contents

The Violin

Prelude

Perhaps you have begun to study the violin. You have chosen a musical instrument beautifully designed and carefully made. Its tone comes fascinatingly close to the human voice. When a violin is well played, its sound is beautiful.

You cannot become a topnotch violinist simply by reading this book, but it may help lead you to a greater appreciation of the art of violin playing and give you a glimpse of the personal rewards that such an accomplishment can bring.

You will find out how a violin is constructed and how its lovely music is made. You will learn where the violin came from in the first place. You will learn about some of the early makers of the violin. You will meet outstanding concert violinists and some violin performers in jazz, and in folk and rock music. You will read of the work of a few outstanding composers of violin music, and you will gain some idea of what to listen for when you hear the pieces they have written. You will learn how to care for your violin and how to have pleasure in playing it.

This book is an introduction; not every single thing there is to know about the violin is in it. For those who wish to read more about music and the violin, other books are listed on pages 113–115.

The more you know about a particular subject, the greater

will be your enjoyment of it—whether it be baseball, football, airplanes, automobiles, dressmaking, cooking, or cats. This is true of the violin, as well. After you have become good friends with it, your violin can be an adaptable, inspiring, and at times comforting, companion all your life.

1. What the Violin Is and How It Makes Its Sound

The violin is the smallest and most highly pitched member in a family of stringed musical instruments played with a bow. Its larger relatives are the viola; the violoncello, popularly known as the cello (pronounced *chel*-lo); and the double bass (pronounced *base*)—also called the contrabass, nicknamed the bass fiddle, and wrongly tagged the bass viol.

The violin's body is a shallow, hollow wooden box, usually fourteen inches long. It is somewhat oval-shaped, and sharply curved in at the waist, which separates two broader areas. The upper area is a little narrower than the lower. The widest part of the top area measures almost seven inches; the widest part of the bottom area is a little more than eight inches; and the narrowest part of the waist measures about four and one-half inches. Violin dimensions vary slightly, according to individual violin makers.

From the violin body's narrower end there extends a short wooden neck, which is usually two-thirds as long as the body. The neck tapers slightly and leans backward. At its top is the head, ornamented with a carved scroll and containing a pegbox. The pegbox holds four sturdy pegs of ebony or rosewood—two on the right, two on the left. Each peg secures a

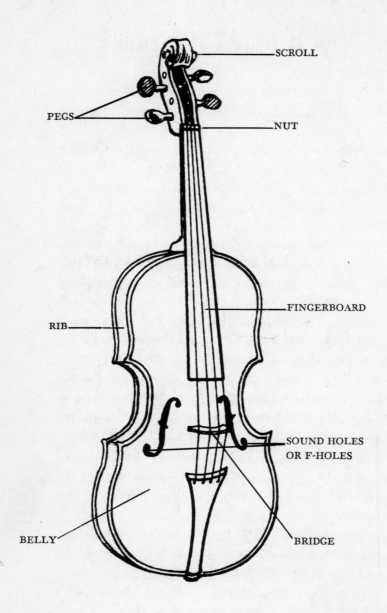

SCROLL

PEGS

NUT

FINGERBOARD

RIB

SOUND HOLES
OR F-HOLES

BELLY

BRIDGE

string that stretches lengthwise on the violin. By turning the pegs, the player can tighten or loosen the strings, so keeping the violin in tune.

From the pegs, the strings pass across a ridge called the nut. Then they stretch along, slightly above a fretless fingerboard, which is glued to the neck. The fingerboard extends partway down the front surface of the box—and suspended slightly over it—to a point just below the top of the waist. Beyond the fingerboard the violin's four strings continue over a low, thin wooden bridge, standing upright a bit below midpoint of the box. At a short distance below the bridge the strings are attached to a long, flat tailpiece shaped like the tongue of a man's high shoe. The tailpiece, made of ebony, is fastened by a loop of gut to a wooden button inserted into the body on its bottom end.

The front of the violin is not flat, but has a slight, graceful bulge, and so is called the belly. The low sides of the box, which join the belly to the back, are called ribs. They are made of six pieces of thin wood, bent and joined together to fit the sweeping curves of the instrument. The back is carefully carved into a slightly arched form made sometimes of one piece of wood and sometimes of two, joined lengthwise down the middle. Inside the violin the ribs are joined and reinforced by blocks of wood at the two ends and at the curving corners of the body. These blocks also make flat surfaces to which the back and belly are glued.

The violin's sound is made by the vibrations of its strings. These vibrations are made louder by the hollow body, which forms a sound box. All stringed instruments are built according to the principle of a single vibrator, the string.

Any sound begins with a slight back-and-forth movement, called vibration. You can see and hear vibrations if you hold your thumb on the tip of the blade of a silver dinner knife so that the handle extends out from the edge of a table, and then pluck the knife's handle sharply with your hand. The knife will shake up and down and make a sound. The faster the vibrations, the higher the pitch, which is the height or depth of a tone.

You can feel sound by just lightly touching your hand to your own throat while you are speaking, or by placing your fingers on a radio, phonograph, or television set that is turned on.

Vibrations disturb the air around them and cause it to move in a series of waves. These waves, called sound waves, spread out in all directions, in somewhat the way that ripples do on the surface of water when an object is dropped into it. But, in the air, the ripples radiate in *all* directions, not just in concentric circles on a flat surface. And of course, the air waves are invisible. When the vibrations of these waves hit the auditory nerves, they are carried to the brain as sound.

A violin string is sometimes vibrated by being plucked or struck, but mostly the violin's sound is made when a bow is drawn across a string. This bow is itself strung with long horsehairs that have been rubbed with rosin to increase their tension. When the bow hairs cross a violin string, they set up a series of rapid shocks that are so regular that the string is kept vibrating. The shocks are made by the string's resistance to tiny overlapping scales on each hair of the moving bow. You can feel these scales if you slide your finger along one of the horsehairs from *tip* to *root*. (From root to tip, the hair feels smooth.)

The bow is strung with each hair alternating—that is, root to tip, tip to root, root to tip, tip to root, and so on—so that the upstroke and the downstroke of the bow will be equal in sound and make a pure, even tone.

"The Koeber," made by Antonio Stradivari in 1725, and detail from an eighteenth-century bow.

The sound of the vibrating violin strings is not very strong in itself; it needs to be amplified, or made louder. The secret of increasing the sound lies in the bridge. It is an elaborately carved piece of wood with a nipped-in waist, and a curved hole cut through the center of its upper part. Its top is also curved, to prevent the player from hitting two strings at once, unless he intends to. The bridge has been carefully designed so that it vibrates freely when the strings that it supports are plucked or bowed. Most of the bridge's vibrations are sent to the belly through the bridge's left, or treble, foot. This foot rests over a narrow strip of even-grained soft pine about 10½ inches long. It is glued lengthwise, slightly obliquely, to the belly's undersurface within the sound box, under the G string. This so-called bass-bar carries the bridge's vibrations to wide areas of the belly. (It also helps the belly support the heavy pressure of the strings on the bridge.)

The bridge's right foot is almost directly over a small cylinder of fine, even-grained wood about one-quarter of an inch in diameter. This cylinder stands upright within the sound box. It is securely fitted between the arches of the belly and the back, and links the violin's upper and lower parts. The French call this sound post l'âme du violin—"the soul of the violin." It collects the vibrations of the various parts of the instrument and helps fuse them together, keeping them continuous and regular with one another. Without the sound post a violin would have a hollow, muffled tone that would not carry far. Much of the shading of a violin's tone depends on how well the sound post is put in place.

The bridge's vibrations, carried by the bass-bar and the sound post to the back and the belly of the violin, cause these parts to vibrate as well, with what is called sympathetic vibration. Since their areas are much greater than those of the bridge or the strings, the original sound is made much louder. This enriching of sound by the sympathetic vibrations of neighboring parts is called resonance.

An elastic material such as wood amplifies by sympathetic vibration and resonance more than an inelastic material such as concrete does. As an example of how resonance works, pinch with your fingers and quickly let go of the prongs of a silver fork as you hold the fork near your ear. The vibrating prongs will make a soft hum. Pinch and let go of the prongs again, but this time touch the end of the fork's handle to a tabletop. The sound will be louder, because the vibrating fork now has caused the tabletop to vibrate. Since the tabletop has more area than the fork, it sets more air in motion, and so makes more sound.

To make a violin's tone softer, a small clamp made of brass, wood, ivory, rubber, or plastic can be placed on the bridge to deaden the resonance. This clamp is called a mute. It looks like a small double comb with three thick teeth. With or without the mute, the musical note is the same; but when the mute is in place it clasps the bridge so tightly that the vibrations are not as strong, and the volume of sound made by the instrument is less.

Nowadays, violinists tend to use a mute, made partly of wire and partly of plastic, that can be permanently attached to the non-sounding part of the strings beyond the bridge. When the violinist wishes, he can simply slide the mute up to touch the bridge to effect the same dampening of sound as that achieved by the old-fashioned mute. Its great advantages are its swiftness of adjustment and the unlikelihood of its being misplaced.

The violin's sound is also built up by the rebounding of vibrations within the sound box. This is a little like having an image reflected back and forth, dozens of times, in a room that has walls lined with mirrors.

The sound of the violin—really the violently disturbed air within its sound box—escapes from it through two graceful slits in the form of small italic letter f's, cut in the belly on either side of the bridge. By humming into one of these so-called f-holes, you can hear and feel the resonance of the sound box. But first, be sure to wedge a handkerchief under the violin's tailpiece to damp out its own vibrations.

The tonal range of a violin covers more than four octaves, beginning with G below middle C and climbing steadily upward. The violin can go through its extraordinary range with astonishing ease. It offers an amazing choice of tone qualities as well as perfect control of pitch—highness and lowness of tone—so that a good player can always be in tune. Except for the human voice, few instruments equal the violin in their power to modify the quality and loudness of a single note. The notes of the violin can be played *legato*, smoothly connected, or *staccato*, distinct from one another. This is one characteristic that the violin shares with many instruments.

The played-upon sections of all four violin strings are exactly the same length. From left to right, when open—that is, when not stopped by the player's fingers—the notes are G, D, A, and E.

A violin is put "in tune" through stretching the strings, by turning the pegs to which they are fastened, to the point at which each string gives out its proper note—G, D, A, or E.

The varying thicknesses of the strings make the notes different. The G is the heaviest string. It vibrates the most slowly—has the lowest frequency—and therefore is the lowest in pitch. The E is the lightest in weight. It vibrates the fastest—has the highest frequency—and is highest in pitch.

Jascha Heifetz waits for his cue.

Thickness is not the only thing that causes variations in the pitch of a vibrating string. Length changes pitch, too. The longer the string, the slower its vibrations and therefore the lower the pitch of the note it will make. To see how this principle applies to the violin, try this experiment. Stretch a thin rubber band around an open-topped box. Pluck the band; it will make a tone. Now pinch it at some point beyond the middle, to make the plucking stretch shorter, and try it again. This time, the tone will be higher.

The violinist does something like this when his finger presses a string to the fingerboard. He is, in effect, shortening the string—making it possible for a smaller section of it to vibrate. He learns from experience exactly where to press the string to make a certain note. By using all four fingers of his left hand in various constantly changing positions on the four strings, he can make many different notes.

Of course, violin playing involves more than finding the proper notes. The interpretation of rhythm (regular beat) and the quality of the tone are two of the things that separate the amateur from the accomplished player. These elements, so necessary to fine performance, depend partly on how skillfully the player uses his bow. It is the bow that brings a violin to life. Bowing creates sustained tone, as opposed to the series of fading tones made by plucking or striking the strings. It makes the violin distinctive.

Another factor in making a distinctive tone is the manner in which the violinist applies his fingers to the strings. The fingertips must be put down firmly and yet—especially on the long notes—leave enough freedom for the left hand to move slightly up and down to produce the "vibrato" which lends life and a singing quality to the tone.

A humorist once described a violinist as "someone who

stretches the guts of a cat over a wooden box and rubs them with the tail of a horse." That is only partly true, for while horsehair is used for bowing the violin, its strings never were from a cat. Gut strings are made now, as they always have been, from the fibrous muscular membranes of lambs' intestines, treated chemically and woven into very strong strands. (The preference is for lambs from dry, mountainous pastures.)

Both the G and D strings are either gut, nylon, or plastic, wound with thin silver, copper, or aluminum wire to make them heavier without making them much thicker. It is difficult to get sound from too thick a string. The A string usually is made of gut or aluminum, the E string is usually made of fine steel or silver wire. It may, however, be of twisted gut, which makes a more colorful tone, but is affected by temperature and humidity.

The violin bow is a springy wooden rod, either round or octagonal, and about 29½ inches long. It is strung with from 100 to 200 white horsehairs, or sometimes with gut threads. The hairs or threads are fastened to the bow's hatchet-shaped head. It is cut in one piece with the stick—a feat of deft and delicate workmanship. The bow's other end is held in the player's hand. This part is called the butt; it is a movable nut, or frog, made of ebony, ivory, or tortoiseshell. When drawn back, the nut tightens the hairs; they are kept in a firm ribbon shape by a small metal ferrule or ring.

2. You and the Violin

Youth is a great advantage to a beginning violinist. Many children begin studying the violin at the age of five. And gifted youngsters—usually those in a musician's family—often start two, or even three, years earlier. For very young players there are specially made small violins, with bows scaled in proportion. There are nine sizes of violin, from full scale through seven-eighths, three-fourths, one-half, one-fourth, one-eighth, one-sixteenth, one thirty-second, to one sixty-fourth of the regular size.

Even in its smallest size the violin is beautiful. To see a violin is to want to hold it in your hands, to own it, to play music so enchanting that the rainiest day will be drenched only with sunshine.

An Italian master violin in the hands of a gifted concert player can bring heaven to earth. The chances are that you will never reach concert perfection or want to. You may not wish to make a career of violin playing. But even though you remain an amateur, your violin will bring you great pleasure.

To be a violinist, you must like music and want to play the instrument you have selected. That is essential. The wish to play must come from inside you. Other people can help by inspiring you and pointing you in the right direction, but it is mostly up to you whether you will become a good violinist or merely someone who squeaks miserably along.

You will need a good sense of pitch. You should know a certain interval when you hear one. An interval is the distance or difference in pitch between tones. If at first you have trouble with pitch, do not give up. Ear training can usually bring you the power to find the notes you seek on the fingerboard. At the famous Toho School of Music in Japan, violin students are given ear training from the time they are three years old.

You may have heard that enormously strong hands and fingers are necessary for playing the violin. It is good to have strength in your hands, but suppleness is much more important. Your fingers need to be flexible in order to handle the strings. Great power is not necessary for pushing a string onto the fingerboard—the distance is short—but a wide stretch in your left hand is essential. Long fingers are a help, but a great spread is better. Your fingers can be short if there is ample spread; many fine violinists have short fingers.

A good exercise for making your fingers stronger and more limber is this. Close them so that their tops rest on the fleshy cushions at their bases. Then slowly extend each finger, one at a time, while you keep the others clenched shut. To develop finger control, hold your extended fingers all together and then separate them from each other, one at a time. Do not worry if at first you have trouble stretching your hand. As you use it more and more, it will loosen up.

If you are right-handed, your violin is held between the jaw and the left shoulder. Normally, your chin should grip to the right of the tailpiece, although if it grips to the left, that is acceptable. Most modern violins are fitted with a chin rest—a shallow affair that looks something like a nut dish or an ashtray.

Itzhak Perlman.

The violin's neck rests between the thumb and forefinger of the left hand—lightly, so that the hand can slide up and down smoothly to reach the various fingering positions. The bow is held in the right hand.

In olden times, violinists held their violins against either the breast or the neck. The violin was not established in the chin position until the eighteenth century, when a firm anchorage was needed for the more advanced fingering techniques that had been developed.

At first, you may have some difficulty with the shoulder and neck muscles that hold the violin between your chin and breastbone. But with time and plenty of practice these muscles will become stronger.

Some teachers are inclined to underrate the need for physical energy and stamina in a violinist. They tell of brilliant students who, during their childhood training period, missed every other lesson due to ailments, and they tell of cripples who learned to play the violin even though bedridden or confined to wheelchairs. (Itzhak Perlman, the talented young Israeli concert violinist, was a childhood polio victim.) But not being able to move the lower part of the body has little to do with how well a person is able to move his arms, shoulders, and fingers.

Handicapped people sometimes have a quality that does help them become good violinists; they have tenacity of purpose—a stubbornness to stick to it. And, because they have lived with a physical problem that cannot be ignored, they have often gone through a good deal of self-examination. From this they may have developed powers of mental concentration—another asset in learning to play the violin. Also important to any student is an ability to understand and make his own whatever he is taught.

A good memory serves a violinist well. This truth was once brought home to James Oliver Buswell IV, an American concert violinist who appears professionally across the nation from fifty to seventy-five times a year. Now in his twenties, he played in a youth concert with the New York Philharmonic Orchestra when he was seven years old. When Buswell was to appear for the first time with Leonard Bernstein, to play the Stravinsky concerto, the conductor asked him, in rehearsal, to change little things at a dozen places in the score. Although the concerto as he had first learned it was already well established in his mind, young Buswell, when he faced the audience that evening, was able to make the requested changes with no difficulty. His memory had risen to the challenge.

A violin pupil needs self-discipline and self-reliance. He must be willing to set aside time for practice and leave other activities that may at that moment seem more attractive.

It is a good idea for students under twelve to have someone sit in at violin lessons to take notes as the teacher uncovers mistakes, then later to see that these are corrected at practice. Ask someone to tell you if you are constantly playing notes flat or sharp; such carelessness may give you what musicians call a tin ear—one that cannot recognize the true musical intervals.

Short and frequent snatches of practice sometimes are better than a long stretch. During practice, see that your violin is in tune, and never try to look at your fingers on the strings.

Do not be discouraged if things go badly at the beginning. At first, probably your greatest difficulty will be in finding the just-right places to press your fingers on the strings to get the right notes, for the violin's fingerboard has no frets

James Oliver Buswell IV.

to guide you. The violin is not like the piano, on which you can press a key to get the same definite note each time. Nor is the violin like the horns, which have valves to press. The motions hardest to master in learning to play the violin are the handling of the bow and the actions of the bowing and fingering hands, which are doing two completely different things at the same time.

You must expect a screeching-string stage at first. Listeners may find that difficult. But remember: This difficult time will pass soon.

It is unlikely you will truly get the feeling of the violin until you have been studying for at least a year—perhaps even two. Then one day the sheer pleasure of playing the instrument will suddenly flow over you. Perhaps it will be when you hear a fine string quartet. Maybe the revelation will come at the concert of an outstanding string orchestra, or better yet, when you are asked to sit in one made of boys and girls your own age. In any case, you will hear the singing strings clearly—perhaps for the first time—as the pure, jubilant spirit of music.

Stay with your violin through the discouragements of the early period of learning. The rewards to come are great and are worth every minute of your effort.

3.   The Violin's Ancestors

The true violin did not appear until about the year 1550. It did not reach its eminent position in the musical world until the late seventeenth century.

The history of the violin's evolution spans a long period of time and is full of romantic nonsense and interesting guesswork. No musical historian can say for sure which ancient instrument was the violin's earliest ancestor. Some claim it was the musical bow, which appears in a few Stone Age cave paintings of before 15,000 B.C. Other musical historians say that the first musical note from a string was the *ping* of some hairy hunter's bowstring in early times. Still others think that the original string note may have occurred when someone accidentally struck the stretched, drying sinews in the shell of a dead tortoise.

Whatever the earliest musical ancestor was, the path from it to the violin of today is long and twisting; its signposts are hard to read; but eventually it leads to the Middle Ages.

During medieval times, cultural ideas began to be traded about. The national peculiarities of stringed instruments gradually merged. From the mingling of bowed and plucked types of instruments the violin finally came.

Each of a variety of instruments influenced the violin's development. Prominent among these instruments were the tube zither; the lute; the cithara, an ancient Greek instrument of the lyre class; the troubadour fiddle, or vielle; and the gittern, or medieval guitar, descended from the cithara. All had bridges, pegs, scrolls, necks, and resonant bodies. The guitar had a narrow waist, round shoulders, and a flattened back. The cithara, the vielle, and the guitar had ribs. In these instruments, for the first time, the back and front resonant plates were separated. Thus a new type of sound box was formed—an improvement over the old vaulted kind that stemmed from the gourd.

It is foolish to credit any one of the early instruments with being the true father of the violin, but the vielle comes closest to filling that role. In it, all the various elements that finally would form the violin came together for the first time.

The vielle was one of the strange new musical instruments brought back to Europe by the minstrels of the Crusades, which began at the end of the eleventh century. The vielle was played mostly as an accompaniment for dances and for the tricks of acrobats, jugglers, and trained wild animals. It was a round-shouldered, ribbed, stringed instrument adapted to bowing and held against the shoulder for playing.

The Spanish developed the vielle into a six-stringed bowed instrument that became known as the viol. When the violin first appeared, the viol was its most serious competitor for public favor.

The viol had an hourglass shape, deep ribs, a flat back, and sloping shoulders. There were frets of gut on its short fingerboard. Lute tuning was used for the viol. Its sound hole was a large ornamental rosette cut into the belly's center. At first, there was no sound post. The viol's tone was heavy and mellow, instead of brilliant. The guitar's playing position —slanted across the body—was used for the viol.

Vielle player of
twelfth-century France;
detail from
Chartres Cathedral.

Woman playing a viol; woodcut from sixteenth-century Switzerland.

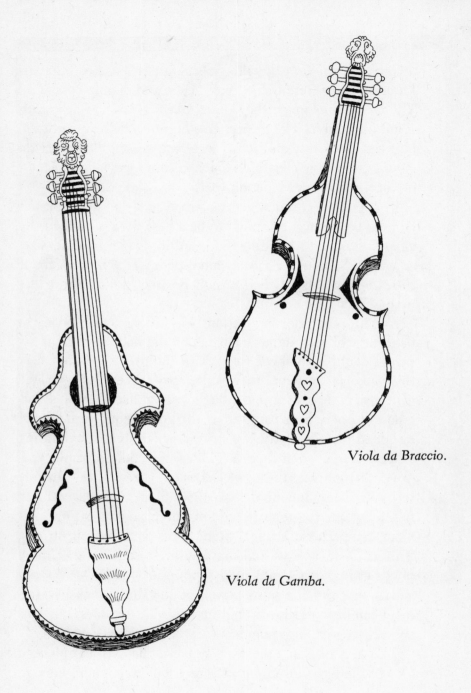

Viola da Braccio.

Viola da Gamba.

The original viol, the alto, was about the size of a guitar. Later offspring were treble, tenor, bass, and double bass viols. The larger sizes made the slanted playing position awkward, if not impossible. The instruments began to be held vertically between the knees and lower legs, and were called *viola da gambas*, meaning "leg viols." Later came *viola da braccios*, or "arm viols," and *viola da spallas*, or "shoulder viols."

In 1600, a new, odd-sized viol appeared—the lyre viol, too large to be a tenor, too small to be a bass. It was dubbed the *viola bastarda*, to indicate its departure from standard size.

Johann Sebastian Bach invented the *viola pomposa*, about the size of a cello. It had a high E string added above the normal four.

Among other viol innovations was the *viol di bordone*, a baritone viol with its neck cut out at the back so that its six strings could be plucked easily with the player's thumb. For this viol, Haydn wrote more than sixty pieces. Its tone was gentle and pleasant, even though a buzz like that of a battalion of angry bees came from the continuous vibration of its added metal sympathetic strings, which were set vibrating independently when their neighbors were bowed or plucked.

Weak tone was the chief defect of the viol, due mainly to its flat back, inherited from the guitar. Viol makers tried to strengthen the tone by adding more bowing strings and more sympathetic strings. Some viols had sixteen strings. Tuning these viols was an exasperating job, for one or more of the strings was continually slipping out of key.

The viol was the most played of the three bowed instrument families present during the violin's early days, but liras and rebecs were also popular.

The liras of that time were not like the classical plucked lyra or the lyre viol just mentioned, but were small enough

Lyre viol made in Italy about 1700.

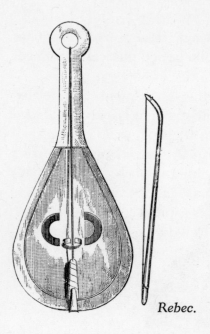

Rebec.

to be held against the chest and played by a long bow. Liras are still played in Greece and also on the Aegean Islands and in Anatolia, the Asiatic part of modern Turkey.

Members of the rebec family were shaped like a skinny pear sliced down the stem. They usually had three strings, and were played like a violin. Normally they had no sound post. The rebec's tone was loud and sharp, with wonderful fiery color.

Rebecs were descendants of an ancient Arabian bowed instrument, the *rebab esh sha'er*, and were in use among the Moors as early as the seventh century. Very likely, the rebab came from a Persian bowed instrument, which in turn was descended from an ancient Indian instrument. The rebec could have been brought to Europe in the eighth century when the Moors conquered Spain, though most historians fix the date of the appearance of a bowed musical instrument in Europe at A.D. 1100.

During the violin's rise to the top a number of related bowed instruments came into the spotlight briefly, then faded away. Notable among them was the *violoncello piccolo*, half as big as the normal cello. For it, Bach wrote *obbligato* parts —parts not to be left out—in nine cantatas.

The *cellone* was a deeper-toned cello.

The *arpeggione* was a small Viennese cello of six strings, tuned like a guitar. It probably would be completely forgotten except for a sonata written for *arpeggione* and piano by Franz Schubert.

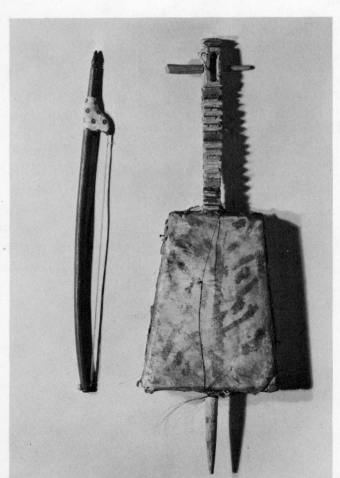

Syrian
rebab esh sha'er.

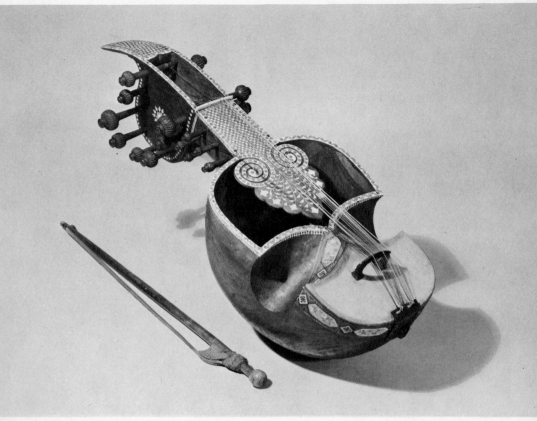

Indian sarangi.

The *octobass* was huge, a double bass 12 feet high, its three strings stopped by means of keys and pedals.

Especially in the East, there are still stringed instruments that have remained the same since ancient times. In India are the *sarangi* and the *sarinda*, unchanged since the days of Baber the Mogul, invader of the Punjab in the sixteenth century. In Oceania are many kinds of one-string instruments and many with three strings. The name of one suggests its own sweet sound: *saw sum sai*. The musical bow is still played on islands of the South Pacific. In Guam it is called the *belimbau-tuyan*.

The crude tube fiddle is found in the Orient and all over Africa. This stringed instrument, played with a tiny bow, has a short cylinder as a sound box; sometimes this box is only a tin can, a gourd, or a hollowed section of a small log. Animal skin stretches over one end of the cylinder; strings run across it and along the round, narrow neck that goes clear through the resonance chamber. The other end of the cylinder is open.

The next time your hear orchestral or violin playing, close your eyes for a moment and let your imagination wander. Drift back in time and listen hard. You may pick up the strains of a plucked bowstring—a sad, thin twanging made by a primitive jungle man. Pay silent homage to him, for without his curiosity back in a time beyond our knowledge, there might have been no such splendid musical instrument as the violin today.

4. Famous Violin Makers

Italy had no bowed musical instruments until the thirteenth century, more than one hundred years after they had spread over the rest of Europe. Yet, from 1550 to 1770, this country was the world's center for the making of fine violins.

An Italian violin maker whom almost everyone, musician or not, has heard about was Antonio Stradivari. He lived in Cremona, in northern Italy, where many fine early Italian violins were made. It is southeast of Milan, on the north bank of the Po River. In the Middle Ages, Cremona was a warlike fortified city. Today its narrow back streets are drowsy and quiet.

The first important family of Cremona violin makers was that of the Amatis. The earliest Amati of prominence was Gotardo, a lute maker, called *il Maestro*, or "the Master," because he was so expert at his work. He had many descendants. Those who became great violin craftsmen were Andrea (1530–1611), first of the Cremona violin makers; his sons Antonio and Geronimo; and Geronimo's son, Nicolò.

In artistry, Nicolò surpassed them all. He lived from 1596 to 1684 and had nine children. Only one, Geronimo II, was interested in violins. He was the last distinguished violin maker of the family.

Nicolò's shop in Cremona, on the Piazza Santo Domenico,

Milan • Brescia •
DUCHY Verona • Padua •
Cremona • Mantua Venice •
Parma • MANTUA
OF MILAN
Genoa • Ferrara •
OF GENOA MODENA Bologna •
REP. OF
• Florence
Pisa • FLORENCE Urbino •
REP. OF
GENOA Siena • Assisi •
(CORSICA) REP. OF PAPAL
SIENA STATES

REPUBLIC

OF

VENICE

ADRIATIC SEA

• Rome

KINGDOM
OF
NAPLES

SARDINIA

Naples •

N

TYRRHENIAN SEA

MEDITERRANEAN

SEA

SICILY

0   50   100   150
Miles

facing Santo Domenico church, had first been established
by his grandfather. There, in the late 1630's, a boy named
Andrea Guarneri became an apprentice to Nicolò Amati.
After Andrea had become a master craftsman, he established
the Guarneri family as violin makers.

Andrea Guarneri had two violin-maker sons: Giuseppe
and Pietro. They handed on their skills to Giuseppe's son,
Pietro II, and to Andrea's nephew, Giuseppe Antonio. Giuseppe Antonio became the family's best violin maker. His
instruments surpass almost all the other early Italian ones.
On the label he put in his violins were the initials I.H.S.,
a symbol for Jesus Christ. Because of these letters, Giuseppe
Antonio became known as Giuseppe del Gesù as his fame
grew. (Gesù is the Italian name for Jesus.) This name distinguished him from the other Giuseppes in the family.
Today, many of the foremost players consider Guarneri del
Gesù violins superior to the finest Stradivari.

Antonio Stradivari was probably not born until 1644, and
so was not one of the pioneer violin makers of Cremona.
He was eleven when he became a beginner in the violin-
making shop of Nicolò Amati. Andrea Guarneri already was
a full-fledged craftsman and was starting his family. Stradivari
worked under Amati for some years. A fellow learner was
Francesco Ruggieri, now considered the finest of that illus-
trious family of violin makers.

In 1667, at the age of twenty-three, Stradivari married a
widow four years older than he, who had one child—a girl.
Five children came of this marriage. Then, by a second marriage, there were four more children. Two of them, Omobono
and Francesco, eight years apart in age, became their father's
assistants.

After the death of Nicolò Amati in 1684, Stradivari opened
his own shop next door to his master's place. It was Stradivari

*Stradivari's house
in Cremona.*

who finally worked out the typical pattern of the Cremona violin. He made subtle changes in measurements that improved the tone. One of Stradivari's first pupils was Giovanni Guadagnini, who became the master violin maker of that family. His father, Lorenzo, had been an assistant to Stradivari. Another of Stradivari's pupils was Carlo Bergonzi, one of the greatest of all violin makers, whose instruments are rated between Stradivari's and those of Giuseppe Guarneri del Gesù.

A few doors from Stradivari's establishment stood the shop of the Guarneris. Other violin makers' workplaces were within walking distance. Most of these people lived over their shops, but a few worked in their living rooms. Some of the men used enormous wardrobe closets for stowing their materials and tools.

"The Eugene Ysaye,"
made by Guarneri del Gesù,
seen from the front,
side, and back.

Painting of a violin maker, believed to be Antonio Stradivari.

Life at that time was slow-paced and simple. The violin builders spent long, tedious hours in creating what are now museum masterpieces. But there were long midday lunches washed down with wine. And when the sun began to sink and the light became too poor for working, the violin makers of Cremona would congregate in a neighborhood tavern. On some days there were picnics, parties, or dances. Shops sometimes were shuttered and locked while the master took his apprentices fishing or to play the outdoor bowling game called *bocci*. There were rainy days when work was suspended because the glue used on the instruments would not dry, and there were holy days when all the shops were closed.

Only a few violin makers would accept payment in advance, because they knew they would be tempted to spend the money. There was no credit. Cash was paid immediately for a finished instrument.

Sometimes the violin makers' children borrowed their fathers' tools, and lost or ruined them. Occasionally a half-finished violin body would be found floating as a boat in a rain puddle. Once in a while, a dog would chase a cat through a shop, upsetting glue pots, scattering violin parts, and creating general havoc. Sometimes a roof would leak onto one of the precious instruments that had been hung in the eaves to dry slowly.

Despite the casual way of life in Cremona, more than

twenty thousand master violins were made there during its golden period.

Other cities of Italy had violin artisans almost as skillful as those of Cremona. Milan, where stringed instruments had been made since 1510, had the Grancino and Testore families. Venice, a crossroads of world trade, offered violin makers the best materials from many foreign lands, and also a wide sales market. In Naples the numerous Gagliano family turned out many excellent violins. Neapolitans said there were "as many Gaglianos in Naples as grains of sand on a beach."

Cremona's greatest violin-producing rival was Brescia, 30 miles to the north. At that time, its cathedral was so prosperous that it employed an orchestra and boasted a spectacular pipe organ.

Among Brescia's many makers of fine violins were Giovanni Battista Rogeri and his son, Pietro Giacomo Rogeri. But the real expert was Giovanni Paolo Maggini. He had been an apprentice of Gasparo da Salò (1540–1609). Da Salò's first violins, adaptations of the *viola da braccio*, are the earliest that have come down to our day. Many experts name him as the maker of the first true violins.

Da Salò's role in the development of the instrument is disputed by the French, who claim the honor for one of their adopted sons, a German, Kaspar Tieffenbrucker. As early as 1510, according to French sources, he is supposed to have made a violin for a royal prince, later Francis I, king of France.

Excellent violins also have come from England, France, and Germany. A prominent violin maker of southern Austria was Jakob Steiner, who had learned his craft in Cremona, Italy. At one time, a genuine Steiner violin cost four times as much as a Stradivari. An outstanding Bavarian violin maker

A quartet of Stradivari instruments. Left to right: cello, viola, and two violins.

was Mathias Klotz, of Mittenwald, in Germany. This was a town of expert wood-carvers, where nearly everyone made violin parts, and many violins were put together by families, with each member working on a part. It is thought that Klotz may have been an apprentice of Nicolò Amati, in Cremona.

Today, thousands of violins are factory-produced. Most of these instruments are used in musical-education programs in public schools. But there are hundreds of individual violin makers, unsung beyond the trade and little known outside their communities. These diligent, honest craftsmen carry on quietly in the Cremona tradition. For most of them, making violins is a means of livelihood; they sell to students and amateurs. Some other people make violins as a hobby. Some doctors and dentists relax in this way. Surgeons and musicians are especially good at making violins because they are adept with their fingers. Among thousands of names listed in an encyclopedia of the world's violin makers from 1550 to the present day are those of bankers, airplane pilots, clerks, scientists, businessmen, advertising executives, artists, writers, actors, and television directors. There are several automobile mechanics, a longshoreman, and a deaf mathematician.

Individual violin makers customarily show pride in their work by gluing a signature label inside the sound box. Usually the labels are small, so as not to interfere with the violin's resonance. Most makers prefer a strip no larger than one by three inches. A label, if there is one, can be seen through the left sound hole. Some of the older labels are handwritten, but most were printed from hand-set type.

A label states the maker's name, the place where the violin was made, and the year it was completed. Many master makers added a special sign or symbol after their signatures. Occasionally a label inscription shows the maker's respect for

Violin labels used by Amati, Stradivari, and Guarneri.

his teacher, or notes that the work was done by apprentices or assistants, *revisto e correto*, "reviewed and corrected," by the master, or *sotto la disciplina*, "under the discipline." The dating of violins has gone on for over four centuries.

Stradivari's labels indicate his frugality. The same lot of printed labels served him for thirty-two years—from 1667 to 1699. Only the first three numerals of the date were printed—166 . The last figure was added by hand during the first years. For the 1670's, Stradivari scratched out the final printed 6 and wrote a 7 in its place, continuing to add the final numeral by hand. For his violins of the 1680's, an 8 was made of the final 6 by closing its top. During the 1690 years the 6 was made into a 9 by erasing its top curl and adding a tail at the bottom. Then Stradivari finally must have run out of labels. The instruments made after 1699 had new labels on which the date was indicated only by the printed numeral 1, with blanks left for the three remaining figures, written by hand. Did he really expect to live through the next century?

He died in 1737, at the age of ninety-three. Stradivari apparently made violins up to the end. During his lifetime his total output of stringed instruments—including violas, cellos, and at least two guitars—was 1,116. About six hundred of these instruments still exist.

Bogus labels have always been a hazard to buyers of master

violins. But even a genuine label does not guarantee an instrument's authenticity; often a label from a ruined master violin has been transferred to a less valuable instrument in order to raise its price.

A buyer should not judge an antique violin by its label alone. He should demand reliable documents and he should thoroughly study the instrument's details of craftsmanship, its wood and varnish condition, its tonal quality, and its general state of preservation. A famous name is useless if the violin is a wreck that cannot produce the kind of music it originally played.

There have always been swindlers in the violin trade. One of the most infamous was an eccentric Italian collector of the early nineteenth century, Luigi Tarisio. He was a violin repairman who had a gift for nosing out antique master violins and slyly trading new and shiny, but vastly inferior, instruments for them. Single-handedly, over thirty years, he took more than one thousand master violins out of Italy and sold them in France, Germany, and England.

When Tarisio died in 1855, two of his nephews inherited his small fortune and his violin collection. Money meant more to them than did violins. They were unsophisticated young men who regarded the priceless instruments as junk. When Jean-Baptiste Vuillaume, one of Tarisio's friends and a shrewd French violin maker and dealer, heard of this he hurried, with all the money he could scrape together, to the nephews' farm at Fontanetto, in Italy. He was able to buy the precious instruments for 80,000 francs—about one twenty-fifth of their true worth. Today, a similar collection would bring close to four million dollars. Among the 144 violins, violas, and cellos in Tarisio's personal collection were twenty-four Stradivaris, three Guarneri del Gesù, four Nicolò Amatis, a viola by

"The Messiah,"
made by Stradivari
in 1716;
front and back views.

"The Hellier," made by Stradivari in 1679. This rare violin is famous for its rich inlay work.

Gasparo da Salò, and rarest of all, Stradivari's incomparable violin known as "the Messiah," a shimmering jewel of an instrument.

Today, prices for Italian master violins begin at about $20,000, but can go to three times that and more. It is a case of supply and demand. There are only so many of these very old, very beautiful instruments. In 1967, the million-dollar Henry Hottinger collection of thirty-six antique master Italian stringed instruments was purchased by Rembert Wurlitzer, Inc., the world's preeminent dealer in master violins. Thirteen of the violins were Stradivaris.

Some master violins too valuable to be on the public market are in museums. One such is Gasparo da Salò's most elegant instrument, richly ornamented with ivory and bronze sculpture and exquisite color, supposedly by the fabulous Florentine artist Benvenuto Cellini. It is now at a museum in Bergen, Norway. A Guarneri del Gesù, once owned by Fritz Kreisler, is now at the Library of Congress, in Washington, D.C. The Ashmolean Museum, Oxford, England, has the most famous of all named master violins, Stradivari's "Messiah."

If a person has doubts in buying a violin, he should get the advice of a reputable dealer or master craftsman. There is at least one in nearly every large American city. For years, in New York City, one of the most respected specialists in the care of the violins of concert artists has been Simone Sacconi, longtime head violin maker at Rembert Wurlitzer, Inc. Sacconi began learning his craft in Venice, Italy, at the age of eight.

The late Luthier Rosenthal, also of New York City, numbered Jascha Heifetz, Mischa Elman, and Efrem Zimbalist among his customers. *Luthier*, in French, means "maker of stringed instruments." Rosenthal's name was really Samuel, but people fell into the habit of calling him Luthier because the sign on his shop door said "Rosenthal, Luthier."

For Mishel Piastro, Rosenthal once restored a Stradivari that had been shattered when a moving man set a heavy lamp on top of its open case. The work took ten days. At the end of that time, Piastro gave a concert with the restored instrument. Its tone was so good that, next day, a prominent music teacher brought a Guarneri to Rosenthal and begged him to break it open and replace its bass-bar with one of his own. Knowing that the original bass-bar was far superior to any he could give the instrument, Rosenthal balked at doing such a foolish thing. But finally, against his better judgment, he gave in, though it broke his heart to disturb the beautiful Guarneri. After the replacement the violin did not have a better tone, but the customer thought it did, because the great Luthier Rosenthal had touched it.

Rosenthal's father had been a noted violin maker in Latvia. As a child of ten, young Samuel had begged to be taught the family trade. His father had promised to begin whenever the boy could provide his own tools. Undiscouraged, Samuel found a railroad tie and dug a spike from it. He propped it on a rail so that when a locomotive rolled by, the spike's end was flattened to form a crude chisel. When he showed it to his father, the elder Rosenthal was pleased by such ingenuity and no longer could refuse his son's request.

Stradivari would have approved of Samuel Rosenthal's father. He knew that anyone who wanted to be a violin maker should be serious about it and should make an early start. It takes years to learn the fine art of making these instruments.

5.   How a Violin Is Made

There are more than seventy parts in a violin. Besides patience and skill in handling delicate materials, a violin maker needs a keen understanding of the science of sound. A violin's tone, rich or poor, depends on how the parts of the instrument react to each other and how they answer the strings' vibrations. A violin maker's goal is to plan the instrument's architecture so well that even the most detailed parts are in perfect balance and cannot be altered without disturbing the whole. The maker cannot allow one resonance to drown out another.

It takes from three weeks to several months to build a first-class violin. Many of the tools for violin making are the same as those for cabinetmaking, or are modifications of them. There are fretsaws, screw cramps, planes, chisels, gouges, flat and curved rasps and files. Some tools were devised especially for violin work. There are small scrapers about three inches wide, of thin, razor-sharp steel, and there are peculiarly shaped knives. Tooth-edged planes and tiny oval ones made of copper, with curved steel blades, are for scooping out the back and the belly. A bending iron curves the violin's ribs. A long-handled mirror, something like the one dentists use, is for looking inside the sound box.

Violins have been made of earthenware, painted and

glazed; leather; papier-mâché; porcelain; and brass, copper, or silver. But these were made to be decorations rather than effective musical instruments.

Wood is the best material by far. It is flexible, yet strong. A violin weighs less than a pound; it must be able to withstand the more than 65 pounds of pressure put on it by the tension of the strings when the instrument is perfectly adjusted.

Today, violin wood has already been seasoned when it comes to a maker. In the old days, craftsmen went into the forest to select their own wood. Stradivari used to tap trees with a mallet, it is said, to determine their pitch.

Ideally, violin wood is from the southern exposure of trees growing on a forest's south side. The best wood is grown on stony soil, as the tree cannot get much water from it. As a result, the tree's trunk grows slowly, and branches do not appear at an early stage of growth. Thus the trunk makes strong, branchless timber—the best for violin bodies.

The most suitable wood for the belly, the bass-bar, and the sound post is Swiss or Tyrolean white pine of a fine, even grain. Ebony is used for the fingerboard, the chin rest, and the tailpiece. Backs are made from curly maple, bird's-eye maple, or pearwood. Violin makers favor unusual markings for the back wood: stripes, flames, curls, or other distinct patterns. Some of Stradivari's most beautiful instruments are said to have been made from maple sent from Dalmatia and Turkey for the making of galley oars, to row the boats of the Italian war vessels. The Turks were often at war with the Italians, so they took care to send wood with an uneven grain. They knew that oars made from it would crack and split under strain in the naval battles with Turkish vessels. But, curly and uneven as the grain was, it was handsome, and the violin makers were quick to buy it for their needs.

Workshop of an instrument maker, eighteenth century.

The trees for violin backs and bellies are ordinarily felled in winter when the trunks are free of sap. The wood is then sawed into sections, and large blocks are cut from them in such a way as to avoid knots and other defects. Sometimes the cut is parallel to the trunk's diameter—"on the slab." More often, the blocks are in a pie-wedge shape, cut along the trunk's radius. Smaller, violin-sized slabs or wedges are cut from the large ones and are stacked so that air and sunshine can get to them. They are left to dry slowly for months, or even years.

The highest artistry in violin making lies in shaping the belly and the back to give them their slight bulges. A high arching of these parts makes the violin's tone brighter and softer. A moderate curvature allows a more powerful tone. The thickness of the belly and the back varies in different areas in order to permit varying vibrations. While working on these parts, the violin maker constantly checks the thicknesses by eye, with gauging calipers, or mechanically with an instrument that registers precisely in inch-fractions or millimeters.

A ticklish job is the application of purfling, the narrow ornamental ribbon—a light-colored stripe finely outlined in black—that edges the violin's belly. It is painted on only the cheapest violins. True purfling is inlaid; it is a thin stripe of light-colored tropical wood laminated to an ebony edging and set into a channel gouged on the belly's surface.

The violin's sound box is completed by adding the ribs that separate the back from the belly. Then the neck, the head, and the fingerboard are added. The bridge, the tailpiece, and the strings are put on the instrument after it has been varnished.

Varnishing, a most important step in building a violin, calls for a sensitive touch on the part of the workman. An oil varnish is the most lasting finish. It must dry very, very slowly in a nonhumid atmosphere. The old masters thought nothing of allowing a month or more to pass between the application of coats of varnish. Their violins often had as many as fifteen coats. The old-time varnishes were colored and toughened by natural resins and dyewood extracts that could be bought in the markets of Venice.

The gentle, sunny climate of Italy was especially good for making violins. The weather conditions not only helped to dry the varnish properly, but also helped to prepare the wood for its first coat. The Italian craftsmen were excellent judges of the exact time when the wood's fibers had opened up but were not yet brittle—the time when varnish would soak into the wood's pores, penetrating lightly and drying, yet leaving the wood still breathing and elastic.

Some violinists say that old master violins sound better than modern ones because of the varnish. That is not so; varnish cannot improve the tone of a violin, although it can ruin an instrument if it is improperly applied. Antique violins have a better tone because their wood is so old that its natural resinous juices have dried up, and as a result tiny resonance chambers within the wood itself have been formed.

Violins have been made in all sorts of shapes: circular, oval, triangular, or guitar-shaped; with domed bodies, two necks, or double bridges and double sets of strings. There have been folding violins and some with glass plates inside their sound boxes, to increase resonance. In America's pioneer days there were roughhewn fiddles made of packing-case wood, flattened lard cans, or even buffalo hide. Some of them are still preserved in museums in the West.

But through all the experimentation and make-do, the best violins have kept the Cremona violin shape. The only changes have been small structural ones made during the early nineteenth century when violinists left small concert chambers for larger halls. Then the violin's neck was angled and lengthened, and the bridge heightened; the fingerboard was made thinner, and the bass-bar longer and stronger, to keep the belly from collapsing under the strings' greater pull. These alterations enabled the violin to be heard better in the bigger auditoriums, and they gave its tone enough volume so that it was not overpowered by the brasses and woodwinds of the enlarged nineteenth-century orchestras.

As for bows, many kinds have been made. But sometime between 1775 and 1790, a Frenchman, François Tourte, and his family—along with Italian composer Giovanni Viotti; a German violinist, Wilhelm Cramer; and an English bow maker, John Dodd—helped standardize the violin bow to its present form and length: 29½ inches.

This new bow was heavier, stronger, and more elastic than previous bows had been. The method of tightening the bow hairs by a screw regulating a movable part was an invention of Tourte's. He gave the bow its elegant *cambré*—the curve inward toward the hairs—and the higher, heavier head that such a change required, to prevent the ribbon of hairs from touching the stick.

The stick itself was made of Pernambuco lancewood imported from Brazil. Tourte found this wood in France, where it was used for industrial dyeing. But for that purpose the worst sort of wood was usually imported; it was cracked, full of knots, and crooked in grain. Tourte had to search through at least 100 pounds of it to find a piece straight enough to use in making his experimental bow.

The new bow had a speedier stroke and was able to produce a smoother *legato*, the joining of one stroke to the next

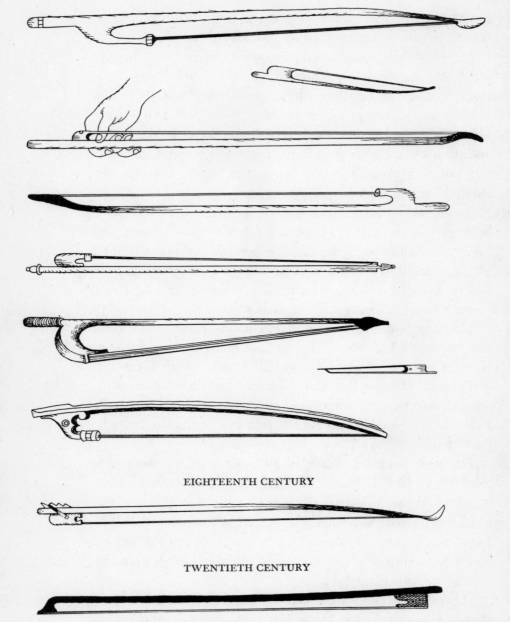

SEVENTEENTH CENTURY

EIGHTEENTH CENTURY

TWENTIETH CENTURY

The evolution of the bow, from the seventeenth to the twentieth centuries.

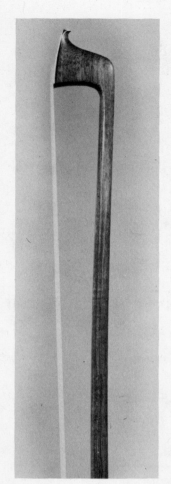 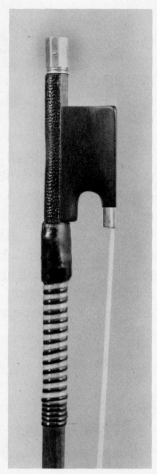

Close-ups of the head (left) and butt (right) of a bow made by François Tourte in Paris, sometime between 1780 and 1790.

without a break. New kinds of bounding strokes and the long *crescendo* (increase in loudness), then becoming popular, were possible with this new bow because it was so flexible and its hairs were so taut. It was capable of giving a strong accent to a single note or chord—an effect called *sforzando*, meaning "forcing."

Recently a bow has been developed made of fiber glass—the same synthetic used for some fishing rods.

If you would like to visit a violin maker's shop, look for listings in the advertising pages of your telephone directory— probably under *Musical Instruments, Repairing*. Usually, violin makers are friendly people. You will find that they are considerate and willing to talk about their work. Call them first, before you visit, so that you will not be bothering them at a busy time. And do not expect them to reveal any of their most precious trade secrets.

6. Professional Violinists

If you do not want to play the violin professionally, but only for pleasure, you are in good company. There have been many distinguished amateur violinists. Among them was Thomas Jefferson. At his home in Monticello he played chamber music with his friends, including Patrick Henry. For musical get-togethers he designed a special four-sided music stand.

Albert Einstein was a better physicist than he was a violinist, but his violin gave him many hours of relaxation. Countless other public figures have eased the stress of their demanding lives by playing the violin.

Possibly an amateur violinist has more fun with his instrument than a professional does. It is not easy to face a large audience, whether it be tolerant or critical. A great deal of concentration is needed to play the violin with other musicians—in a string quartet or trio; in the pit orchestra of a theater or an opera house; but especially in a major symphonic organization.

With a group, however, the stress of playing in public is not so great as that felt by a concert solo violinist. His worst moment of tension comes at his first entrance onstage. Even the most seasoned professionals never completely conquer the nervousness caused by facing for the first time that sea of faces, the audience. Usually, release from tension does not come until the first time the performer leaves the stage. Then, when he returns, the master violinist finds that he is at ease for the rest of the concert.

Tension begins to build long before the concert. Concerning the trials of a concert day, famed violinist and conductor Alexander Schneider has this to say: "You sleep badly the night before. Then, in the morning, you check your instrument and you find the strings, which you had already changed a few days before, are bad and the instrument doesn't sound so good. So you try to run to the violin maker for help. If he knows you well, he pretends he is touching something, and suddenly the fiddle sounds well and strong and the strings are all right. If he is not interested or is not a good friend, he'll tell you the truth—that he can't help you. So then you go back home and start changing strings. It's all an illusion— all in the mind."

From the moment a violinist awakens on the day of an evening concert he is on edge. In the morning comes rehearsal with the orchestra or an accompanist. Then, following a big midday meal, the violinist may go to bed and try to sleep for a couple of hours—or at least to relax. When he gets up, he may take a long shower or a hot tub, and then practice. At dusk he may have a cup of tea, but possibly nothing else. Concert violinists seldom eat dinner until after a performance.

Today, the living pace of concert violinists is much swifter than in the past. More engagements are played, with little time between them; one hundred appearances a year are not unusual. Travel to and fro is by jet plane; it is not leisurely journeying by train or by ocean liner, as it used to be. In summer, countless music festivals, in the United States and abroad, lure concert artists. Veterans of the concert world cannot see how young violinists are able to keep up so swift a pace and still find time to mature musically.

Jascha Heifetz recently told a newspaper interviewer, "Of course, I played a great deal when I was younger, but there was always time for reflection. We had time between engagements, no matter how many we filled, to think, to study music, and read books. Hardly anyone now takes off a few weeks to rest, study, and think—let alone a whole summer, as we used to do."

James Oliver Buswell IV, mentioned earlier in this book, is in his early twenties—not in his sixties, as Heifetz is—and so he can afford a cooler view of today's concert-circuit tempo. Young Buswell does not consider his fifty to seventy concerts a year a difficult schedule. He points out that Isaac Stern plays as many as one hundred and fifty. But then, Stern is not going to college. When he was interviewed for this book, Buswell was on the dean's list—the honor list—at Harvard College. During the height of the concert season—early February through March—Buswell usually plays a concert every other day, hopping between cities by air.

He says: "It's not so much a matter of energy, but of getting enough rest before a concert. About schoolwork, well, there are lots of times at college when you have nothing, or not much, to do, so it's a matter of doing what you have to do in a reasonably short space of time. You get pretty good at organizing things. Then, I have no concerts in May at all, so that gives me time for any catching up in my studies."

Years ago, Russia provided most of our young violinists. In imperial days, violin playing offered a way out of the Jewish ghetto. Many young violinists now come from Israel, Korea, and Japan. An astonishing sight in Tokyo is an annual recital

Isaac Stern.

of youthful violinists in which two thousand players perform in unison.

Most concert violinists own and play instruments built by the old Italian masters. Many of these violins are named for the people for whom they were made, or for former owners. James Oliver Buswell IV has the "Leveque," a Stradivari named for the French nobleman who once owned it. Isaac Stern has two Guarneris—one, the "Eugene Ysaye," named for a renowned Belgian violin virtuoso. In large concert halls, Jascha Heifetz plays his Guarneri del Gesù, the "Ferdinand David," dated 1742 and named for the teacher of master violinist Joseph Joachim. In smaller halls, Heifetz uses a Stradivari.

Violin player Zino Francescatti has the "Hart" Stradivari, named for George Hart, once a prominent London violin dealer. Nathan Milstein and David Oistrakh play Stradivaris. Itzhak Perlman, a spectacular young Israeli violinist, favors an early Guarneri. The well-known Korean violinist Young-Uck Kim has Stradivari's "Koeber," dated 1725.

One of the early pioneers to develop string-playing technique was the great Claudio Monteverdi, who in 1607 composed the earliest opera still in the repertoire—*La Favola d'Orfeo*. Monteverdi claimed to be the first composer to use the *tremolo* and *pizzicato* for special effects, and while some scattered earlier examples of these techniques may be found, Monteverdi was certainly the first influential composer to make use of them. The tremolo is produced on the violin with rapid short strokes of the bow on the same note, the pizzicato, by plucking the strings instead of using the bow. Monteverdi instructed the players to use two fingers in plucking the strings instead of one, as is more customary today.

One of the first violin virtuosos—and the very first to gain

Arcangelo Corelli.

an international reputation through his compositions—was Arcangelo Corelli (1653–1713) , who spent most of his life in Rome, where he was greatly beloved and the friend of cardinals and princes. His contribution did not lie so much in the development of new playing techniques as in the dignity and deep emotion displayed in his music and his performance of that music, particularly in the slow movements. He knew how to make the violin really sing, and one can appreciate this fact when listening to his sonatas for one or two violins and to his *concerti grossi*. (A *concerto grosso* is a composition for a small group of instruments playing alternately with a large group.) All of these compositions are still often played, both in the concert hall and on records. Corelli's most famous piece, *La Follia*, is of such beauty that accomplished violinists do not disdain to play it, even though it is technically quite within the range of an average third-year violin student.

Claudio Monteverdi.

Although Corelli composed no concertos for solo violin, pitting a single instrument—instead of a small group of instruments—against an orchestra, some of his near contemporaries invented and developed this popular form. The first to do so were Giuseppe Torelli of Bologna (1658–1709) and Tomaso Albinoni of Venice (1671–1750). But the greatest of them all was the Venetian Antonio Vivaldi (1675–1741), whose work shows a great technical advance over that of his fellow composers. A red-headed priest, he became music master for a foundling school for girls, where he developed a first-class orchestra. For his students, he composed fifty violin concertos (not to mention four hundred for other instruments), and today quite a few of them, including the popular group of little concertos called *The Four Seasons*, are still heard in our concert halls.

One of the greatest violin virtuosos of the mid-eighteenth century was Gaetano Pugnani (1731–98) —short, misshapen, and ugly, with a large nose like a jib topsail. Pugnani's first appearance on any concert stage always caused smothered laughter. But when he poured forth his brilliant runs, his double- and triple-stops, audiences were left breathless—and respectful of his enormous ability.

Pugnani was an even greater teacher than performer. His star pupil was Giovanni Battista Viotti (1755–1824). Viotti is considered the ancestor of many of the twentieth-century concert violinists, for this reason: He taught Jacques Pierre Joseph Rode, who in turn was the teacher of Joseph Böhm. A pupil of Böhm's, Jakob Dont, was the violin master of Leopold Auer, whose pupils in turn included some of the brightest violin stars of the twentieth century: Mischa Elman, Jascha Heifetz, Nathan Milstein, Mishel Piastro, and Efrem Zimbalist.

Antonio
Vivaldi.

Gaetano Pugnani.

Giovanni Battista Viotti.

In 1782, sixteen years before Pugnani died, Nicolò Paganini was born in Genoa, Italy. He became the most dashing violin virtuoso of all time, a super-showman of instrumental technique.

Paganini used every known technique—and invented others not known before. He played not only melodies but swift runs in octaves and even in tenths; he would play a melody on one string and accompany it, guitar-like, by plucking lower strings with his little finger; he produced cascades of fireworks by bouncing his bow in swift alternation with left-hand pizzicatos. Other violinists had experimented with artificial harmonics—that is, producing very high notes by placing one finger firmly on the string and another, lightly, on the same string, a fourth above it. But Paganini played whole melodies' this way *on two strings at once.* To woo one of his many lady loves he composed a sentimental duet to be played on the E, or highest, string (representing the lady) and on the G, or lowest, string (representing Paganini) at the same time. He also composed a great many pieces for the G string alone.

Some of these effects—and many more—are employed in his famous twenty-four *Caprices,* which today's virtuosos still struggle with. But the caprices are not merely tricks; the last of them has so much musical meat in it that Schumann, Liszt, Brahms, and Rachmaninoff have all written major piano works based on it.

Wherever he appeared, Paganini usually had to play five or six concerts in succession. In London for a five-concert series, he was forced by public demand to give fifteen "final" concerts.

Vienna worshiped Paganini. As a public idol he outshone even the giraffe presented to the Viennese court by the Pasha of Egypt. After Paganini's arrival in Vienna, souvenirs *à la*

A Paganini concert, 1804.

giraffe gave way to those honoring the famous violinist. There were also violin-shaped pastries and Spaghetti Paganini.

Paganini had extra-sharp hearing. He felt physical pain whenever anyone spoke loudly near him. He could hear faint whispers at a great distance. His ear for music was so sensitive that he could play completely in tune on a violin that was completely out of tune.

He played the mandolin when he was five, the violin when he was seven. By then, he could sight-read any music. At eight, Paganini composed his first violin sonata; at eleven, he gave his first public concert. From his fourteenth to his seventeenth year, Paganini practiced ten hours daily, with only a pet spider for company. He learned the important works of the greatest violinists from Corelli to Viotti.

Every really great violinist has made an early start on the violin. Fritz Kreisler was admitted to the Vienna Conservatory of Music when he was seven, although the minimum entrance age at that time was usually fourteen. Yehudi Menuhin's first violin lesson came when he was four. At six, he made his public concert debut, and at ten he appeared for the first time in New York's Carnegie Hall, the goal of all violin virtuosos, playing the Beethoven Concerto with the New York Philharmonic led by Arturo Toscanini.

Jascha Heifetz, son of a theater orchestra violinist, began studying the violin at the Royal Music School in Vilna, Russia, when he was five. One year later, at a public concert in Kovno, he played the Mendelssohn violin concerto with amazing self-assurance. At eight, he played for the master teacher Leopold Auer, then professor of violin at the St. Petersburg Conservatory of Music, and was enthusiastically invited to enter the school.

At that time, Jewish people were not allowed permanent

Leopold Auer.

Fritz
Kreisler.

Mischa Elman (standing) with Eugene Ysaye (seated).

residence in St. Petersburg. An exception was made for conservatory students, but not for their families. Accordingly, Jascha's father was forbidden to stay with his son. Auer got around this ban by also making a pupil of the elder Heifetz, then aged forty.

When he was sixteen, Jascha Heifetz made his American debut at Carnegie Hall. He performed so well that when Mischa Elman, dabbing at his brow during the intermission, remarked to the famous pianist Leopold Godowsky, "Rather warm in here, isn't it?" Godowsky replied, with a wicked grin, "Not for *pianists*."

As a concert instrument the violin reaches the peak of musical artistry, but it has not lost its common appeal. Fiddlers are still favorite music makers at weddings, christenings, dances, and barn raisings. There are still traveling fiddling minstrels. Circus clowns and nightclub and television comedians still build laughs with a violin. The instrument is played at country picnics, fairs, and church gatherings. Comic fiddlers make music from the backs of galloping horses, on tightwires, and on unicycles. With their strings and bows, violinists still imitate birds and beasts, just as Carlo Farina did in 1627 with his *Capriccio stravagante*, in which the violin was made to sound like barking dogs, fifes, drums, and a strumming guitar.

There have been excellent jazz violinists, and there still are. Joe Paoli was one of the first, playing in King Oliver's Creole Jazz Band back in 1921. With the old John Handy band was Mike White.

No jazz buff can ever forget the irreverent gusto of Stuff Smith's electrically amplified violin. A top trumpeter named Ray Nance, with Duke Ellington's band, was also a fine violinist. So is Joe Venuti, who played with Paul Whiteman and

Red Nichols, who has headed up his own groups, and who is still, in his mid-seventies, traveling the world over as the best-known jazz violinist in history.

A great jazz violinist today is Sven Asmussen, of Denmark. An exciting new French jazz violinist is Jean-Luc Ponty. Overseas, Stephane Grappelly remains the dean of jazz violinists. His jazz improvisation of the first movement of Bach's *Concerto for Two Violins*, a recording made with Eddie South—known as the Dark Angel of the Violin—was considered by Nazi occupiers of Paris to be so horrible an example of what they considered degenerate art that they burned the entire edition, they thought. But forty copies were safely hidden; they are now collectors' items.

Violins are being introduced into hard-rock groups. These rock instruments have built-in electronic pickups instead of traditional sound boxes. Of our modern balladeers, the Beatles were among the first to use the violin—in 1965, when a Paul McCartney ballad, "Yesterday," was accompanied by a string octet.

Many violinists outside the concert hall are found in country music. The most successful fiddler in that area is Roy Acuff, whose violin, along with his singing and song writing, has made him a multimillionaire. Another great country fiddler is Bob Wills, who can be counted on to draw audiences of thousands, even in sparsely populated areas.

The whole country music craze actually began with a fiddler—bald and bearded, eighty-one-year-old "Uncle Jimmy" Thompson, who in November, 1925, scraped out an hour of hoedown tunes, jigs, and reels on the first barn dance program of a local radio station, WSM, in Nashville, Tennessee. The program started that city on the road to being the country music capital of the world.

Nowadays country fiddling is done close to the bridge, with the fiddle held very near to an amplifier's microphone. The sound is loud, sharp, and clear.

The automobile and the radio brought folk fiddling out of the Appalachian Mountains. As it has gained recognition the music has been changed to satisfy popular taste. To hear the folk tunes in their noncommercial purity, a person would have to go back into the highlands of the Carolinas. There, in rude cabins snuggled into the hills, are stouthearted, hard-bitten folks who are direct descendants of America's early Scottish, Irish, and English settlers. The ballads and fiddle tunes from their original homelands have been preserved almost intact through the generations. In this backwater land, fiddlers still are regarded with the respect given the minstrels of feudal times. To hear these hill people play is to glimpse the earlier days of violin performers, when there was no such thing as a concert hall. Their numbers, however, are dying out. Efforts have been made to preserve their work on recordings, before it is gone forever and the old songs are forgotten.

7.   Violin Music and Its Composers

For more than a century after its creation the violin was looked on as an inferior musical instrument. At first, hardly any music was written especially for it. Most music of that time was designated for "all kinds of instruments," or for one or another of several similar instruments—for instance, "for lutes and viols." It was rare to find "violino" specified. But violins were sometimes used to double for voice parts.

Although the first book of sonatas for solo violin was published in 1640, violin music was composed mainly for the ballet part of an opera or as an overture for a court pageant until about 1700. There were no commercial solo concerts for paying audiences until 1725. There were only the musicales that aristocrats held formally for their guests in their drawing rooms, gardens, or courtyards.

The golden age of the Italian violinist-composers was from 1720 to 1750. Among those inspired by the two great virtuosos Corelli and Torelli was Antonio Vivaldi of Venice, mentioned in the preceding chapter as the composer of fifty violin concertos.

Giuseppe Tartini of Padua, born almost twenty years after Vivaldi, was even more prolific. He turned out over two hundred violin concertos, almost as many sonatas, and fifty variations on a theme by Corelli.

Other fine violin composers of that period were Pietro Locatelli, Pietro Nardini, Francesco Veracini, and Giovanni Battista Martini, a Franciscan monk of Bologna. Owner of a 17,000-volume music library, Martini was a master of counterpoint—that is, the art of placing two or more related but independent melodies to play against each other.

Pugnani and Paganini, the leading violin virtuosos of the late eighteenth and early nineteenth centuries, also composed many violin works. Paganini's *24 Caprices for Unaccompanied Violin* are especially praiseworthy. Another superlative composer of the time was Viotti. He poured out an avalanche of violin music, including 51 duos, 29 concertos, 21 string quartets, and 18 sonatas. An especially active composer of chamber music in that day was Luigi Boccherini, the court composer to Friedrich Wilhelm II of Prussia. For strings, Boccherini composed 141 quintets, 99 quartets, 65 trios, and 6 sextets. He also composed 25 quintets for the flute with strings, as well as sonatas and duets for the violin and other instruments.

In the amount of music written, no musicians of any other nationality have come close to the early Italian composers for the violin. Not all their music was good, for their compositions often were made on demand, to honor some special occasion or to please a patron. Some of their pieces were played only once, then forgotten. Much of that early music, however, has survived and is treasured today.

In Germany, during this Italian upsurge of violin music, Johann Sebastian Bach (1685–1750) was busy composing orchestral pieces and religious choral works, and writing for his great love, the organ. But he found time to compose also for other instruments. For a single violin he wrote two concertos. He also wrote a concerto for two violins; one for flute,

Luigi Boccherini.   *Johann Sebastian Bach.*

violin, and a keyboard instrument; six sonatas and six suites for unaccompanied violin; and six sonatas for violin and keyboard instrument accompaniment. (Since the piano was in its infancy in Bach's day, keyboard accompaniments were written for earlier instruments, such as the harpsichord.)

The influence of Italy was much more marked in the music of Bach's contemporary, George Frideric Handel (1685–1759). Born and trained in Germany, Handel traveled to Italy, where he fell under the spell of the Italian violin masters. In the course of his long life, Handel poured out a stream of violin music, including 18 concerti grossi and 17 violin sonatas.

In Austria, Franz Joseph Haydn (1732–1809) enriched violin music by composing 83 string quartets; 31 trios for piano, violin, and cello; 66 trios for two violins and bass; 8 violin sonatas; and 3 concertos for violin and orchestra.

Wolfgang Amadeus Mozart (1756–91), another Austrian and unquestionably the greatest of the eighteenth-century composers, wrote, at the age of eighteen, five fine violin concertos for his own use on a concert tour. For although he later became the finest pianist of his day, he was also a violin virtuoso when still in his teens. His very large contribution to chamber music literature includes 23 string quartets (the last 10 of which are still performed by every professional and amateur group), 5 string quintets, and numerous pieces for strings and piano, including no fewer than 34 sonatas for the violin.

In the early part of the nineteenth century, Ludwig van Beethoven (1770–1827) composed a concerto for piano, violin, and cello; a string quintet; 16 quartets; 4 string trios; a serenade for flute, violin, and viola; 10 violin sonatas; 2 romances for violin and orchestra; and his Violin Concerto in D Major, opus 61, one of the finest of all violin concertos. He also composed nine trios for violin, cello, and piano.

Ludwig van Beethoven.

The interior of a nineteenth-century concert hall.

Felix Mendelssohn.

Johannes Brahms.

Felix Mendelssohn (1809–47), born the year of Haydn's death, wrote pieces for three, four, five, six, and eight stringed instruments. His Concerto in E Minor, opus 64, for violin and orchestra is popular with concert artists. Mendelssohn's *Scherzo* from the Octet in E-flat for Strings, opus 20, written when he was only sixteen, is a superb piece for eight stringed instruments; it is light and *pianissimo*—or very soft—all the way.

In the latter half of the nineteenth century, Johannes Brahms (1833–97) wrote a violin concerto and one for violin and cello; two sextets; two quintets, and three quartets for strings; a trio for violin, horn, and piano; three trios for violin, cello, and piano; three violin sonatas; and three quartets for piano and strings.

The twentieth century has produced some wonderfully stirring violin music from three Russian composers: Aram Khachaturian (1903–), Sergei Prokofiev (1891–1953), and Igor Stravinsky (1882–). Stravinsky's *In Memoriam Dylan Thomas*, written in 1954, for choral group, four trombones, and string quartet, is delightful.

Among other modern composers for the violin were Paul Hindemith (1895–1963), Béla Bartók (1881–1945) (his six string quartets are stunning), and Arnold Schönberg (1874–1951), who experimented a great deal with violin, other instruments, and voice. Walter Piston (1894–), longtime teacher of composition at Harvard University, composes for the violin, and so does Peter Mennin (1923–), president of the Juilliard School of Music in New York City.

Every composer writes violin music in his own particular style. But each uses the characteristics of the instrument to get various effects. Watch for these effects when you listen to the music.

Paul Hindemith.

Béla Bartók.

Aram Khachaturian.

The many ways of bowing produce different sounds. Bowing over the fingerboard (*sul tasto*) makes a soft, mellow tone, without luster. A glassy, brittle tone comes from bowing near the bridge (*sul ponticello*). A violin's natural harmonics are overtones, in high-register, made by lightly stopping a vibrating string at one of its exact fractional points, as that of a half, third, fourth, or fifth; the sound is flutelike and is called *flautando* or *flautato*.

Bouncing the bow lightly on the strings is called *saltando*, or "leaping." *Glissando* is a gliding effect made by sliding a finger along a string as it is bowed. Striking strings with the wood of the bow is called *col legno*. Plucking them with the fingers is called *pizzicato*. *Colla punta d'arco* is playing with the point of the bow. When the bow makes heavy up-and-down strokes without leaving the string, that is called *martellato*, or "hammered." Bowing with the nut or heel of the bow is called *am frosch* or *au talon*. Playing a note or succession of notes as briefly as possible is called *staccato*; when this is done so that the bow leaves the string between notes, it is called *spiccato*.

Tremolo is the fast repeat of a tone by a quick up-and-down movement of the bow. A trill, a birdlike sound, is made by a fast switch between a tone and its upper neighbor. The notes of a chord played rapidly one after the other, rather than all together, make an effect known as *arpeggio*. *Vibrato* is the swaying of a note by a trembling motion in the playing hand and the finger that is stopping the string.

Learning to listen to violin music, or any other kind of music, with intelligence and appreciation, is a skill you must develop for yourself. However, a knowledgeable person or a written text can help you to identify certain passages in a musical composition as they occur in a live performance or recording. Recognizing and being able to evaluate the various technical aspects of the music will help you in comprehending what the composer and the performer are expressing through their art.

To appreciate music, you must know its language well. That knowledge can come only from a great deal of listening. Learn to relate each segment of the music to what follows it. Remember that music has appeal for both the senses and the intellect.

Every musical tone has pitch (highness or lowness) ; duration (longness or shortness) ; intensity (softness or loudness) ; and tone color, or timbre. Tone color is the quality of a tone —that is, thin, thick, light, dark, sharp, dull, smooth, rough, warm, cold, velvety, fuzzy, rounded, or perhaps something else. Each of the four characteristics of tone—pitch, duration, intensity, and timbre—is important, and all of them combine to make a musical note.

Different notes arranged by a composer in patterns of time are what make music. It has melody, rhythm, tempo, and harmony.

Melody is a succession of notes that have some relation to one another and form an artistic whole. Almost all music has melody, though often it is well hidden.

Rhythm is based on the regular occurrence of a beat in music. The beat itself is generally known to musicians as the metre. Tempo is the rate of speed at which a rhythmic pattern is played. The composer of a piece of music indicates its tempo as *adagio*, very slow; *andante*, moderate speed; *allegro*, fast; *vivace*, lively and faster; *presto*, very fast; *prestissimo*, as fast as performers are capable of playing. These words, and others like them, are Italian terms that have become traditional in music.

Harmony is the arrangement of chords—tone patterns made by playing two or more notes at the same time—into a whole that has some structure or plan. Consonant chords, made up of notes at certain intervals, sound restful and seem to be tonally satisfying. Dissonant chords, made up of notes at certain other intervals, sound restless and incomplete, demanding something more to follow them.

The patterns of melody, rhythm, tempo, and harmony are held together by the musical composition's form—the master plan of the piece. Will it be a symphony, an opera, a concerto, or just a simple love song? Other words for form are "structure" and "design." To bring interest and variety to musical form, patterns of melody, rhythm, and harmony are repeated and contrasted with one another, and tones are made to vary in color, intensity, duration, and pitch.

The forms in which the solo violin most often appears are the sonata, a composition in several movements for a single instrument (or for solo instrument and pianoforte), and the concerto, a composition for orchestra and one or more solo instruments—usually only one. The concerto calls attention to the virtuosity of the solo instrument's performer.

Usually there are three movements in a concerto. Traditionally, the first movement is fast. Just before it ends, a brilliant solo called a *cadenza* is customarily inserted. It is full of flourishes that enlarge on the basic melodies set forth in the work. Cadenzas often are by some composer other than the original one, or are sometimes by the soloist himself.

A concerto's second movement is slow and lyrical, and is often in song form; sometimes it is a theme—a leading melodic pattern—with its variations, which are musical embroideries on the original melody.

The closing movement is lively, most often in *rondo* form

—that is, with sections that repeat themselves between contrasting melodic patterns.

In a symphony, composed for the instruments of an orchestra, many violins play together. A symphony generally is in four movements. The form of the first two movements is the same as for the concerto, but without the cadenza. The symphony's third movement may be either a minuet or a scherzo —Italian for "joke"—a light, fast-paced, whimsical piece of music. Some scherzos are masterpieces of musical wit. The finale, or final movement of the symphony, may be in rondo or theme-and-variations form.

Strings are perhaps the most important group of a symphony orchestra. Generally there are twice as many stringed instruments as other instruments. Most large symphonic organizations have almost sixty stringed instruments—about thirty violins, ten violas, ten cellos, and eight double basses. The violins are divided into two sections: first violins to the left of the conductor; second violins to the right—although sometimes they are placed in other ways.

A symphony member, if asked, is likely to tell you that the difference between playing first and second violin is the pay. Or he may say that the second violin is not a musical instrument at all, but a condition of servitude, because second violins usually perform the less exacting, less exciting parts, acting as an inner voice and a rhythmic help. Usually they play the melodic line only when they join the first violins in moments of climax.

The strings are often heard alone in orchestral compositions. Some composers have written symphonic compositions entirely for strings. Mozart did, in his Serenade in G, *Eine Kleine Nachtmusik* (A Little Night Music) , and so did Tchaikovsky, in his *Serenade in C for Strings*.

Some listeners believe the string quartet to be the purest and highest form, not only of chamber music, but of all music. A piece for string quartet—two violins, a viola, and a cello—often follows the form of the symphony, but does not have its dramatic effects, its great waves of sound, or its tumble of tone color.

Chamber music has room for essentials, but no padding. The music brings out precisely what the composer intended, sometimes with humor, but without bombast. It is gentle music, sometimes called the music of friends.

When he sees string players of chamber music for the first time, a music student almost always feels let down. There is no great spread of musicians and their instruments, but only a handful of players at stage center, each reading his own music, and without a leader.

Most often, one instrument carries the melody while the others furnish a sort of embroidery effect, or they may play against the melody. An audience must learn to listen for the quality of tone, for clear sonority, as the players blend and answer each other in their music, with each player as important as the others, and with a fine disregard for virtuosity by all, except as a means of expressing a thought.

An appealing movement in string quartet music is the *Andante cantabile* from Tchaikovsky's Quartet No. 1 in D Major, opus 11. It is a Russian folk song, played with wistful tenderness on muted strings.

When you go to the opera, listen to the strings in the orchestra as well as to the singers onstage. The singers' words are echoed by the strings; the silences of the strings heighten dramatic effects. The *tremolo* creates suspense; the *pizzicato* is used to point up mystery, wit, or agony. Passages played *sul ponticello*, on the bridge, are comic; those played *col legno*, with bow stick on strings, are either humorous or sinister.

Because their tone is duskier than that of the violin, violas are used when the action is guarded, or in situations of menace. Cellos play in moments of lament or of angry passion— such as murder or execution. In its upper register, the double bass can suggest horror. This instrument is able also to sing of real grief. In Ruggiero Leoncavallo's opera *I Pagliacci*, after Canio, the clown, has finished his lament, "*Vesti la giubba*," all the strings taper off to leave the basses in the lowest part of their range sobbing the heartbreaking melody to the bitter end.

After you have been to many symphony concerts, string quartet recitals, and the opera, you are likely to agree that, of all musical instruments, the violin is one of the best for listeners, because its emotions range so widely. It can dance and flirt. It can be friendly, haughty, or hostile. It can be brilliant just for the sake of brilliance. It can be sad and soulful one minute; the next, it can be a happy buffoon, ready for the wildest gymnastics. Yet it can be trusted with the most sacred and serious matters. The violin can speak of love and hate, of life and death, without being embarrassing. It is never boring.

8. The Care of Your Violin

You cannot give your violin too much attention. Without constant care, it will not make very good music.

Keep your instrument away from excessive heat. Heat will make the wood brittle. Always beware of extreme changes in temperature.

Keep your violin away from cold and dampness. They can take all the life from your instrument. Dampness is invited into your violin by an accumulation of lint and dust in the sound box. Get rid of that dirt once a year by pouring dry, slightly warm, but *not cooked*, grain cereal into the sound box through a sound hole. Shake it carefully around. Be gentle, lest you displace the sound post. Then pour out the cereal.

Keep the violin's outer surface polished and free of rosin dust. To eliminate scratches, rub them with the *meat* of an almond nut. Be sure the outside scratchy skin of the nut has been removed.

Always handle a violin by its neck, but do not let grease, grit, and dirt gather there. Keep your violin well wrapped in a soft cloth and safe in its case when it is not in use. Keep the case closed.

Do not put your violin on a high shelf or in any other place from which it may fall, with damaging results. Do not lay it in any spot where someone can sit or step on it, or stumble over it. Remember that a tuned-up violin is under heavy pressure from its strings. A hard bump or a drop to the floor may be disastrous.

Use only the most exact gauge of strings. Tune them to pitch gradually. Overstretching tends to break strings or to loosen the winding parts. Strings should be cleaned to remove sweat left by your fingers. Keep your fingernails short so that they do not cut the strings.

Change strings *one at a time*, and be careful not to take the pressure off the bridge entirely or it may topple and break or cause the sound post to be displaced. Watch out for this also when tuning.

Whenever a bridge is replaced, it should be carefully fitted by an expert violin maker, for it is very important to the proper sound of your violin. The bridge's feet should be shaped to the belly's contour, and the arch should be cut to match that of the fingerboard. Too high a bridge will raise the strings so far above the fingerboard that the fingers cannot press them down without difficulty.

If the fingerboard develops humps, have them straightened. If the pegs stick or jump, take them out one at a time and rub them with peg composition, which can be obtained at a music store. If the pegs are worn, get a new set.

A violin bow should be handled with great care. The bow's head is the part most often broken. Any shock received by the bow's butt is sent through the hairs to the head, and may crack it.

Do not touch the bow hairs with your fingers or let anything greasy get on them. Never tighten the hairs to the point of pulling the stick out of *cambré* into a straight line. Be sure to wipe the rosin off the stick each time you finish using the bow.

When the bow is not in use, keep it in the violin case to protect it from atmospheric changes and other hazards. Before you put it away, loosen its screw, to relieve the strain on its head.

Smooth bow hairs should be replaced promptly, as they will cut down on the violin's tone. The same goes for broken hairs. A bow stick will become warped whenever enough hairs are lost to cause a change of tension.

Above all else, be wary of incompetent violin repairmen. Always get a man who is recommended by someone you trust. Clumsy hands, carelessness, indifference, or ignorance sometimes have turned a beautifully made violin into a mere worthless wooden box with strings on it.

Finale

The rewards of violin playing are rich and varied. First will come the satisfaction of having mastered a difficult musical instrument—a most pleasant feeling. Tedious hours of practice, finger pains, and muscle aches will be forgotten once you have learned to make notes come out the way you want them to, putting them together as the composer meant them to be.

Once you have conquered the technical problems of violin playing, you will doubly appreciate the artistry of professional concert violinists. A concert will give you more pleasure than ever before.

Reading about the violin and studying the lives of famous players and composers, past and present, can be a pleasant pastime or an absorbing hobby for you.

Collecting records of violin music will greatly increase your understanding of the instrument you have chosen to play. With records, you can stage concerts for your family and friends right in your own living room.

With a violin, the dimensions of your life will increase; your horizons will broaden. Your violin will be a passport into the world of music and an introduction to the very interesting people who live there. You will find boys and girls, men and women, with interests similar to your own. You will make new friends. Some of them you may continue to know for the rest of your life.

Perhaps you will join your school orchestra and learn the joy and discipline of making music with others. Maybe you will want to go to one of the musical summer camps that are so much fun. You will find them at the seashore, in lake country, and high in the mountains. There is an especially good one at Aspen, Colorado, in the Rocky Mountains.

A book, *The Parent's Guide to Music Lessons*, by Wills and Manners (Harper & Row) , carries a handy listing of more than two hundred of these music camps located in forty-six states. Up-to-date listings of music camps can be had from the Association of Private Camps, 55 West 42nd Street, New York, N.Y., or the American Camping Association, 342 Madison Avenue, New York, N.Y. For camps abroad sponsored by the International Federation of Music Youth, write to Jeunesses Musicales, Palais des Beaux Arts, Rue Baron Horte, Brussels, Belgium; or to Jeunesses Musicales du Canada, 430 St. Josephs Oueste, Montreal, Canada. For other music camps in Canada, write to the Canadian Culture Information Centre, 56 Sparks Street, Ottawa, Canada.

With other young musicians, you may want to form a small neighborhood string symphony orchestra. Or, as a less ambitious project, you might join with others in playing chamber music. It is a wonderful experience in fellowship. A string quartet is something that must be done with other players or it cannot be done at all. The players *make* music—the pure, jubilant spirit of it. They do not just play it. Life and music come together and there is no difference between them. It is beautiful.

Your group might even become good enough to get engagements at local clubs, meetings, dinners, and parties. See if you can arrange musical evenings at your local library. Visit children's hospitals and old folks' homes to bring *live* string music to persons who seldom hear any.

Perhaps your progress with the violin will be so great that you will want to compose for it. What pleasure to create a short solo, a sonata, a string quartet—even a concerto!

You could make a career of violin playing, though not everyone is gifted enough. But even if you become only a so-so player of the violin, you will still have gained much just by having studied it. As long as you stay with your violin you will continue to grow and to know how truly beautiful the world can be when you make music.

Glossary

ACCORDATURA—The tuning scheme of a musical instrument; thus, the *accordatura* of a violin is G-D-A-E.

ADAGIO—Slow, an indication of tempo used as a playing direction in music.

ALLEGRO—Fast, lively, an indication of tempo used as a playing direction in music.

AM FROSCH—*See* Au talon.

ANDANTE—Going, moving, a moderate tempo—used as a playing direction in music.

ARPEGGIO—The playing of the notes of a chord rapidly, one after the other, ripplingly, instead of playing them all together.

AU TALON—Bowing with the nut, or heel, of the bow. Also called *am frosch*.

BASS-BAR—A narrow strip of wood glued lengthwise to a violin belly's undersurface within the sound box, under the G string.

BELLY—The front, or upper, surface of a violin.

BOW—A wooden rod with horsehairs stretched from end to end, used in playing instruments of the violin family. *Butt*, the end held in a player's hand; *head*, the free end; *nut*, or *frog*, the movable part at the butt end that tightens the bow hairs when it is drawn back.

BOWING—The manner of using the bow in playing a violin or a similar stringed instrument. *See also* Arpeggio, Au talon, Colla punta d'arco, Col legno, Glissando, Martellato, Pizzicato, Ricochet, Saltando, Spiccato, Staccato, Sul ponticello, Sul tasto.

BRIDGE—A low, thin, carved piece of wood that stands upright on a violin's belly a bit below its midpoint. It supports the strings and conducts their vibrations to the violin's sound box.

BUTTON—A small wooden disk that is inserted into a violin's body at its lowest point; the tailpiece is attached to the button.

CADENZA—In a concerto, a brilliant, unaccompanied solo section—once improvised, now more often already composed. It enlarges on the themes set forth in the work and exhibits the player's technique.

CAMBRÉ—The inward curve of the wooden part of a violin bow toward the hairs.

CAPRICE—A whimsical musical work of free, irregular form, usually lively in style. (Also called *Capriccio*.)

CHAMBER MUSIC—Music of an intimate sort and for a small number of players, suitable for performance in a small room —as opposed to music composed for a church, theater, or a large hall.

COLLA PUNTA D'ARCO—A musical direction indicating that the violin's strings are to be played with the point of the bow.

COL LEGNO—A musical direction indicating that the violin's strings are to be struck with the stick of the bow.

CONCERTO—A large-scale musical composition for orchestra and one or more solo instruments. The word comes from the Latin *concertare: con*, meaning "with," and *certare*, meaning "strive"—the whole meaning "to strive with."

CORPUS—The shallow, hollow wooden box that is a violin's body.

COUNTERPOINT—The arrangement of two or more related but distinctive melody lines, played together to achieve a definite harmonic effect.

COUNTRY MUSIC—The field of American popular music that embraces rural and provincial tunes.

CRESCENDO—Increasing in tone, getting louder—used as a playing direction in music.

DOUBLE-STOP—Two notes played simultaneously on a violin.

DUO—A duet; a musical composition for two players or two voices.

F-HOLES—Two graceful slits in the form of small italic letter f's, cut through a violin's belly on either side of the bridge. Also called sound holes.

FINGERBOARD—The wooden facing (usually ebony) that is glued to the front of a violin's neck. The fingers of a player's left hand press the instrument's strings down on the fingerboard at various given points, and so change their length and pitch.

FLAUTANDO. *See* Flautato.

FLAUTATO—The flutelike sound made by stopping a vibrating violin string at one of its exact fractional points (as that of a half, a third, a fourth, a fifth, and so forth).

FORM—The master plan for putting together melody, rhythm, tempo, and harmony to make a musical composition, be it symphony, opera, sonata, concerto, duet, trio, quartet, quintet, or something else. The basic elements in musical form are repetition, variation, and contrast.

GIMPING—The process of winding a violin string with fine wire to lower the tone by increasing the weight of the string without making it too much thicker.

GLISSANDO—In a sliding manner—the effect accomplished by running the finger rapidly over a violin string.

HARMONY—The structure of a piece of music in terms of its chords and the way they relate to one another.

HEAD—The very top of a violin—that part beyond the fingerboard.

INTENSITY—In music, the softness or loudness of a musical tone.

LEGATO—A musical direction indicating that notes are to be played in a smooth, connected manner; the opposite of *staccato*.

MARTELLATO—Italian for "hammered"—a musical direction indicating that the violin is to be bowed with detached and strongly accented up-and-down strokes.

MELODY—A succession of musical notes having a definite relationship one with another and forming a meaningful whole.

MINUET—A slow, stately seventeenth-century French dance for groups of couples; written in triple time.

MOVEMENT—A distinct section of a larger musical composition, having its own key, rhythms, structure, and themes. A movement is more or less self-contained, but is not necessarily independent of other movements of the piece of music.

MUTE—A small clamp that is placed on a violin's bridge to muffle the tone.

NECK—The short, narrow, tapering wooden shaft that extends from the top of a violin's body.

NUT—A strip of ebony at the pegbox end of the fingerboard of a violin. The nut keeps the strings raised slightly above the level of the fingerboard.

OCTAVE—A succession of eight notes comprising a scale, the

eighth one having twice as many vibrations per second as the first; also, the interval between the lowest and the highest of these notes.

OCTET—In music, a composition for eight voices or instruments.

PARTS OF A VIOLIN—See Bass-bar, Belly, Bridge, Button, Corpus, F-holes, Fingerboard, Head, Neck, Nut, Pegbox, Pegs, Ribs, Scroll, Tailpiece.

PEGBOX—The open-fronted box at the top of the violin's neck, into which pegs are inserted.

PEGS—Sturdy pins of wood to which a violin's strings are attached and which may be turned to tune the instrument.

PIANISSIMO—Very soft in volume, used as a playing direction in music.

PIANO—Soft, used as a playing direction in music; also refers to the keyboard instrument of that name.

PITCH—The relative highness or lowness of a musical tone.

PIZZICATO—A musical direction indicating that the strings of the violin are to be plucked with the fingers.

PRESTISSIMO—As fast as an instrumentalist is able to play— used as a playing direction in music.

PRESTO—Very fast, used as a playing direction in music.

PURFLING—A thin strip of light-colored tropical wood, laminated to an ebony edging and set as an inlay into a channel gouged on the surface of a violin's belly.

QUARTET—In music, a composition for four voices or four instruments.

QUINTET—In music, a composition for five voices or five instruments.

RESONANCE—The reinforcement of sound by the vibration of something other than the original vibrator.

RESONANCE CHAMBER—A sound box.

RHYTHM—The organization of music in respect to accent and time; the regular occurrence of beat.

RIBS—The low sides of a violin's box that join the belly to the back.

RICOCHET—A musical direction indicating that a bounding, or skipping, staccato is to be played by the bow on the strings. More often called *Spiccato*.

RONDO—A form of instrumental music in which a principal melody alternates with other, contrasting, melodies.

SALTANDO—A musical direction indicating that music is to be played with the bow bouncing lightly on the strings in a rapid staccato.

SCALE—A series of tones within an octave which are used as the basis of musical composition.

SCHERZO—Italian for "joke"; a light, fast-paced, whimsical short piece of music.

SCORDATURA—An abnormal tuning of a stringed instrument, generally to make possible the playing of unusual passages.

SCROLL—The ornamental carving on the head of a violin or other bowed string instrument.

SEXTET—In music, a composition for six instrumentalists or voices.

SFORZANDO—A musical direction meaning "forcing"—giving a sudden strong accent to a single note or chord.

SONATA—A musical composition in three or four movements, usually for one or two instruments.

SOUND BOX—A resonance chamber, a hollow box that serves to reinforce vibration.

SOUND POST—A small cylinder of wood that stands upright within a violin's sound box, directly under the bridge's right foot. Securely dry-fitted between belly and back, the sound post links those two harmonious plates elastically.

SPICCATO—*See* Ricochet.

STACCATO—A musical direction indicating that notes are to be held as briefly as possible, and detached from one another.

STRING QUARTET—The playing combination of two violins, a viola, and a cello.

SUL PONTICELLO—A musical direction indicating that the violin's strings are to be played by bowing near the bridge.

SUL TASTO—A musical direction indicating that the violin's strings are to be played by bowing over the fingerboard.

SYMPATHETIC VIBRATION—The vibrations produced in one body by vibrations in a neighboring body. The vibrations in both bodies occur at exactly the same intervals.

TAILPIECE—A long, flattish brace of ebony, shaped like the tongue of a man's high shoe; it anchors the violin's strings below the bridge.

TEMPO—The rate of speed of a musical composition.

TIMBRE—The quality of a musical tone: thin, thick, light, dark, sharp, dull, smooth, rough, warm, cold, or something else.

TONE COLOR—*See* Timbre.

TREMOLO—A fast repeat of a tone by quick up-and-down movement of the bow.

TRILL—A rapid alternation of a note with the one just above it in the scale.

TRIO—In music, a composition for three instruments or three voices.

TRIPLE-STOP—A chord made by playing on three strings at once.

TRIPLET—A group of three notes played in the time of two of the same value.

VIBRATION—The rapid back-and-forth, often invisible movement in space of an object against which some force has been applied.

VIBRATO—The swaying of a note by a trembling motion in the violin hand and the finger that is stopping the string.

VIVACE—Quick and lively—an indication of tempo, used as a playing direction in music.

Suggested Books for Reading and Reference

Violins and Violinists

BOYDEN, DAVID D. *The History of Violin Playing.* New York: Oxford University Press, 1965.

FARGA, FRANZ. *Violins and Violinists.* London: Rockliff, 1949. (Obtainable in U.S.A. from The Macmillan Co., New York.)

HILL, W. HENRY, ET AL. *Antonio Stradivari, His Life and Work.* New York: Dover Publications, Inc., 1963.

JALOVEC, KAREL. *Italian Violin Makers.* New York: Tudor Publishing Co.

NORTON, M. HERTER. *The Art of String Quartet Playing.* New York: W. W. Norton & Company, 1966.

WHEELER, OPAL, AND GILLETTE, H. S. *Paganini, Master of Strings.* New York: E. P. Dutton & Co., 1966.

Musical Background

BEKKER, PAUL. *The Orchestra.* New York: W. W. Norton & Company, 1963.

BENADE, ARTHUR H. *Horns, Strings and Harmony.* (Anchor Books.) Garden City, N.Y.: Doubleday & Company, Inc., 1960.

BERNSTEIN, LEONARD. *The Infinite Variety of Music.* New York: Simon & Schuster, Inc., 1966.

CLEMENCIC, RENÉ. *Old Music Instruments.* New York: G. P. Putnam's Sons, 1968.

COPLAND, AARON. *Copland on Music.* New York: W. W. Norton & Company, 1963.

GOLDRON, ROMAIN. *Ancient and Oriental Music.* (History of Music Series, vol. 1.) Garden City, N.Y.: Doubleday & Co., Inc., 1968.

MACHLIS, JOSEPH. *Music: Adventures in Listening.* New York: W. W. Norton & Company, 1968.

McKINNEY, HOWARD D., AND ANDERSON, W. R. *Discovering Music.* 4th ed. New York: American Book Company, 1962.

MOORE, DOUGLAS. *Listening to Music.* New York: W. W. Norton & Company, 1963.

ROBERTSON, ALEC, ED. *Chamber Music.* Baltimore: Penguin Books, Inc., 1957.

SELIGMANN, JEAN, AND DANZIGER, JULIET. *The Meaning of Music: The Young Concertgoer's Guide.* New York: World Publishing Company, 1966.

SLONIMSKY, NICOLAS. *The Road to Music.* New York: Dodd, Mead & Co., 1966.

Reference Books

BAINES, ANTHONY, ED. *Musical Instruments Through the Ages.* Baltimore: Penguin Books, Inc., 1966.

BAUER, MARION, AND PEYSER, ETHEL. *How Music Grew.* New York: G. P. Putnam's Sons, 1939.

————. *Music Through the Ages.* Ed. by E. E. Rogers. New York: G. P. Putnam's Sons, 1967.

DONINGTON, ROBERT. *The Instruments of Music.* (University Paperbacks.) New York: Barnes & Noble, 1962.

GEIRINGER, KARL. *Musical Instruments: Their History in Western Culture from the Stone Age to the Present.* Ed. by B. Miall. New York: Oxford University Press, 1945.

JALOVEC, KAREL. *Encyclopedia of Violin-Makers.* 2 vols. Ed. by P. Hanks; tr. by J. B. Kozak. New York: Tudor Publishing Co., 1968.

SACHS, CURT. *The History of Musical Instruments.* New York: W. W. Norton & Company, 1940.

WESTRUP, J. A., AND HARRISON, F. L., EDS. *The New College Encyclopedia of Music.* New York: W. W. Norton & Company, 1960.

A Sampling of Violin Recordings

The following list of recordings is a sampling of the finest of the wide range of violin music available on records. You will find some selections from the basic repertoire, as well as less familiar compositions. Both types of music are rewarding for the attentive listener. The records listed are single LP's, unless otherwise noted. Multi-record sets have been included if they feature performances of special merit or historical importance, or if they contain desirable performances that are unavailable on a single LP. The listings are drawn from the Schwann Catalog, the standard guide to Long Playing records, which is issued monthly.

Many schools have facilities for listening to records, and a growing number of libraries have records available for loan. If you hear a performance that you'd like to own, investigate whether it is available on an inexpensive recording. Some of the leading record companies have budget labels that feature excellent performances and good sound at low prices. Whenever possible these inexpensive labels have been included in this discography.

Classical

BACH, JOHANN SEBASTIAN (1685–1750)

Chaconne (from Partita No. 2 for Unaccompanied Violin) ; Broekmann. Decca 79955.

Concerto in D Minor for Two Violins; D. and I. Oistrakh, with Royal Philharmonic under Goossens. Deutsche Grammophon Gesellschaft (DGG) 138820.

Two Concertos for Violin, S. 1041/2; D. Oistrakh, with Vienna Symphony. Deutsche Grammophon Gesellschaft (DGG) 138820. (Coupled with preceding entry.)

Sonatas and Partitas for Violin, Unaccompanied; Arthur Grumiaux. Philips 2-900 (2-record set) .

Three Sonatas for Viola da Gamba and Harpsichord; Dupré, Dart. Oiseau-Lyre 50161.

BEETHOVEN, LUDWIG VAN (1770–1827)

Concerto in D for Violin and Orchestra, opus 61; Heifetz, with the Boston Symphony Orchestra under Munch. RCA Victor LSC-1992.

Quartet No. 9 in C, opus 59, "Rasumovsky"; Lenox Quartet. Dover 7240.

Quartet in E-flat for Piano and Strings, opus 16; Horszowski, with members of the Budapest Quartet. Columbia MS-6473.

Romances Nos. 1, 2, for Violin and Orchestra, opus 40, 50; Menuhin, with Philharmonia Orchestra under Furtwängler. Seraphim 60135.

BOCCHERINI, LUIGI (1743–1805)

Quartets: in D, opus 58, No. 5; *in F,* opus 64, No. 1; *in D,* opus 64, No. 2. Carmirelli Quartet. Music Guild S-123.

BRAHMS, JOHANNES (1833–97)

Concerto in D for Violin, opus 77; Oistrakh, with Orchestra of the National French Radio under Klemperer. Angel S-35836.

Quartet No. 1 in C Minor, opus 51/1; Amadeus Quartet. Westminster 9019.

BRITTEN, BENJAMIN (1913–)

Simple Symphony for Strings, opus 4 (1934); English Chamber Orchestra under Britten. London 6618.

DVOŘÁK, ANTONIN (1841–1904)

Quintet in A for Piano and Strings, opus 81; Curzon, with Vienna Philharmonic Quartet. London 6357.

ENESCO, GEORGES (1881–1955)

Sonata No. 3 in A Minor for Violin and Piano, opus 25; Y. Menuhin (violin), H. Menuhin (piano). Angel S-36418.

FRANCK, CÉSAR (1822–90)

Sonata in A for Violin and Piano; Stern (violin), Zakin (piano). Columbia MS-6139.

HANDEL, GEORGE FRIDERIC (1685–1759)

Concerti Grossi, opus 6; Y. Menuhin, with Bath Festival Orchestra. Angel S-3647 (4-record set). . . . . Schneider, with Schneider Chamber Orchestra. RCA Victor LSC-6172 (3-record set).

Water Music; Y. Menuhin, with Bath Festival Orchestra. Angel S-36173.

HAYDN, FRANZ JOSEPH (1732–1809)

Concerto No. 1 in C for Violin; Menuhin, with Bath Festival Orchestra. Angel S-36190.

Quartet in D, opus 64, No. 5, "*Lark*"; Hungarian Quartet. Turnabout 34062.

Quartet in C, opus 76, No. 3, "*Emperor*"; Amadeus Quartet. Deutsche Grammophon Gesellschaft (DGG) 138886.

KHACHATURIAN, ARAM (1903–   )

Concerto for Violin and Orchestra (1940); D. Oistrakh, with Moscow Radio Symphony under Khachaturian. Melodiya-Angel S-40002.

MENDELSSOHN, FELIX (1809–47)

Concerto in E Minor for Violin, opus 64; Stern, with Philadelphia Orchestra under Ormandy. Columbia MS-6062.

Octet in E-flat for Strings, opus 20; Dalley, Laredo, Schneider, Steinhardt (violins), Rhodes, Tree (violas), Parnas, Soyer (cellos). Columbia MS-6848.

MOZART, WOLFGANG AMADEUS (1756–91)

Concerto No. 1 in B-flat for Violin and Orchestra, K.207; Grumiaux, with London Symphony under Davis. Philips 900236.

Concerto No. 5 in A, "The Turkish," K.219; Stern, with Columbia Symphony Orchestra under Szell. Columbia MS-6557.

Quartet in F for Oboe and Strings, K.370; Soloists of Berlin Philharmonic. Deutsche Grammophon Gesellschaft (DGG) 138996.

Quintet in A for Clarinet and Strings, K.581; De Peyer, with Melos Ensemble. Angel S-36241.

Serenade No. 6 in D "Serenata Notturna," K.239; English Chamber Orchestra under Britten. London 6598.

Sonatas for Violin and Piano, K.301, 304, 376; Druian (violin), Szell (piano). Columbia MS-7064.

Trio in E-flat for Viola, Clarinet, and Piano, K.498; De Peyer, with Melos Ensemble. Angel S-36241.

PROKOFIEV, SERGEI (1891–1953)

Concerto No. 1 in D for Violin and Orchestra, opus 19; D. Oistrakh, with State Radio Orchestra under Kondrashin. Monitor S-2073.

RAVEL, MAURICE (1875–1937)
Tzigane for Violin and Orchestra; Perlman, with London Symphony under Previn. RCA Victor LSC-3073.

RESPIGHI, OTTORINO (1879–1936)
Sonata in B Minor for Violin (1917); Heifetz, Bay. RCA Victor LVT-1034.

SCHUBERT, FRANZ (1797–1828)
Octet in F for Strings and Winds, opus 166; Vienna Octet. London 6051.

Quartet No. 14 in D Minor, "Death and the Maiden"; Juilliard Quartet. RCA Victor LSC-2378.

Quintet in A for Piano and Strings, "Trout," opus 114; Koeckert Quartet. Deutsche Grammophon Gesellschaft (DGG) 136488.

Sonata in A for Violin and Piano, opus 162; D. Oistrakh and Oberin. Dover 5245.

STRAVINSKY, IGOR (1882–)
Elegie for Unaccompanied Violin or Viola (1944); Trampler. RCA Victor LSC-2974.

TCHAIKOVSKY, PETER ILYITCH (1840–93)
Concerto in D for Violin and Orchestra, opus 35; Heifetz, with Chicago Symphony under Reiner. RCA Victor LSC-2129. . . . D. Oistrakh, with Philadelphia Orchestra under Ormandy. Columbia MS-6298.

VITALI, TOMMASO ANTONIO (1665–?)
Chaconne for Violin; Heifetz. RCA Victor LM-2074. . . . D. Oistrakh. Monitor 2042.

VIVALDI, ANTONIO (1678–1741)
Concerto in D for Two Violins and Lute; Breitschmid, Lemmen, Stingl, with Württemberg Chamber Orchestra under Faerber. Turnabout 34153.

Concerto in A Minor for Flute, Two Violins, and Continuo; London Harpsichord Ensemble. Nonesuch 71004.

Concerto for Four Violins and Orchestra. Y. Menuhin, Masters, Goren, Humphreys, with Bath Festival Orchestra. Angel S-36103.

Concerto for Trumpet and Violin; André, Artur, with Rouen Chamber Orchestra under Beaucamp. Philips World Series 9049.

Concerto for Violin, Cello, and Orchestra; Heifetz (violin), Piatigorsky (cello), with Chamber Orchestra. RCA Victor LSC-2867.

The Four Seasons, opus 8, Nos. 1–4; Ricci, with Stradivarius Chamber Orchestra. Decca 79423.

WEILL, KURT (1900–50)

Concerto for Violin and Woodwinds, opus 12; Gerle, with Vienna Wind Group under Scherchen. Westminster 17087.

A Recording for Historical Reference

Glory of Cremona; Ricci. Decca DXSE-7179.

Virtuoso Performance Recordings

Concert Encores; Heifetz. RCA Victor LM-1166.
Immortal Performances; Kreisler. RCA Victor LM-6099.
Virtuoso; Suk. Epic BC-1367.

Index

126